C000038720

Why Academic Freedom Matters

Why Academic Freedom Matters

A response to current challenges

Edited by Cheryl Hudson and Joanna Williams

CIVITAS

First Published July 2016

© Civitas 2016
55 Tufton Street
London SW1P 3QL

email: books@civitas.org.uk

All rights reserved

ISBN 978-1-906837-82-2

Independence: Civitas: Institute for the Study of Civil Society is a registered educational charity (No. 1085494) and a company limited by guarantee (No. 04023541). Civitas is financed from a variety of private sources to avoid over-reliance on any single or small group of donors.

All publications are independently refereed. All the Institute's publications seek to further its objective of promoting the advancement of learning. The views expressed are those of the authors, not of the Institute, as is responsibility for data and content.

Designed and typeset by
lukejefford.com

Printed in Great Britain by
4edge Limited, Essex

Contents

Part Two: The University in the Twenty-First Century

Part Three: Threats to Academic Freedom

Acknowledgements

My thanks to the many friends and colleagues, on campus and off, whose commitment to rigorous debate and fearlessness in exploring challenging ideas sustains me. Some of them are contributors to this volume. Thanks are especially due to Joanna Williams, my co-editor, for providing a place at the Centre for the Study of Higher Education, University of Kent in which to think and talk about the many issues addressed here. I am indebted to the University of Liverpool's history department, a wonderfully collegial place to work through my ideas about history and higher education. I dedicate this book to my sons Frank and Orlando in the hope they always keep their minds free.

Cheryl Hudson

Thanks are due to the University of Kent's Centre for the Study of Higher Education for hosting the conference *Academic Freedom: Still Relevant in Today's Universities?* in March 2015. This conference brought together some of the contributors to this volume and very much inspired its creation. Thank you to *Spiked* for putting the issue of free speech on campus so firmly on the public agenda. Thank you to Cheryl Hudson for being not just a great co-editor but more importantly, an intellectual collaborator. Above all, thank you to my husband, Jim Butcher, and children, George, Harry and

Florence, for not complaining about the weekends I've spent in front of a computer!

Joanna Williams

Contributors' Biographies

Joanna Williams is the author of *Academic Freedom in an Age of Conformity: Confronting the Fear of Knowledge* (Palgrave Macmillan 2016) and *Consuming Higher Education: Why Learning Can't Be Bought* (Bloomsbury 2012). She is the education editor of *Spiked* and a Senior Lecturer in Higher Education at the University of Kent. Joanna regularly contributes to national higher education debates and her research has been published in a number of academic and popular journals.

Cheryl Hudson is University Teacher in History at the University of Liverpool. Cheryl has taught at universities in the UK and the US and is former director of the academic programme at the Rothermere American Institute, University of Oxford. Her research interests lie in the history of American political culture and she has published articles in a number of academic and popular journals. Cheryl is co-editor of *Ronald Reagan and the 1980s* (2008). Her current book project is *Citizenship in Chicago: Race, Ethnicity and the Remaking of American Identity, 1890-1930*.

Philip Cunliffe is Senior Lecturer in International Conflict at the University of Kent. He blogs at *www.thefirstphilippic.wordpress.com*. His most recent book, *Legions of Peace: UN Peacekeepers from the Global South* was published in 2013.

Thomas Docherty is Professor of English and of Comparative Literature at the University of Warwick, having previously held the Chair of English at Trinity College Dublin, and Chair of English at the University of Kent. He is the author of many books, including, most recently, *Universities at War* (Sage 2014); *Confessions: The Philosophy of Transparency* (Bloomsbury 2014); *For the University* (Bloomsbury 2012); *Aesthetic Democracy* (Stanford 2008); and *The English Question* (Sussex 2007).

Kathryn Ecclestone is Professor of Education at the University of Sheffield. Kathryn's research explores the ways in which endemic public, political and professional concern about 'emotional well-being', 'resilience' and 'vulnerability' has encouraged the huge spread of ideas and practices from diverse areas of therapy, counselling and psychology across the education system, changing the teacher/academic/student relationship, support systems and what counts as appropriate curriculum knowledge.

Rania Hafez is Senior Lecturer and Programme Leader for the MA Education at the University of Greenwich. She is also co-chair of the Learning & Skills Research Network, London & South East and was previously Director of Post Compulsory Education at the University of East London. Rania has researched and published on teacher education, teacher professionalism and on Islam and education. In 2008 Rania founded the professional network 'Muslim Women in Education'. In addition to her academic work Rania Hafez is a regular political and cultural commentator.

Dennis Hayes is Professor of Education at the University of Derby and the Director of the campaign group *Academics For Academic Freedom* (AFAF) which he founded in 2006. He was a columnist for the *Times Educational Supplement* and is a member of the editorial board of the *Times Higher Education* magazine and a columnist for *The Conversation*. In 2009 he edited and contributed to a special edition of the *British Journal of Educational Studies* on academic freedom and he writes regularly in the national and international press on free speech and academic freedom.

James Heartfield is author of *The Death of the Subject Explained*, and an historian of the British Empire. His book *Who's Afraid of the Easter Rising?* was published by Zero Books in 2015.

Jenny Jarvie is an independent news and culture writer who reports from Atlanta for *The Los Angeles Times*, and writes on cultural issues for publications including *The New Republic, ArtsATL, CityLab*, and *The Atlanta Journal-Constitution*. Born in London and based in Atlanta, she has worked as a staff writer at *The Los Angeles Times* and *The Sunday Telegraph*.

Tara McCormack is Lecturer in International Politics at the Department of Politics and International Relations, University of Leicester.

Alan Ryan is Emeritus Professor of Political Philosophy at Stanford University and former Warden of New College, Oxford.

Anthony J. Stanonis is Lecturer in modern US history at the Queen's University Belfast. He is author of *Creating the Big Easy: New Orleans and the emergence of modern tourism, 1918–1945* (2006) and *Faith in Bikinis: American Leisure and the Coastal South* (2014) and editor of *Dixie Emporium: Tourism, Foodways, and Consumer Culture in the American South* (2008).

Jason Walsh is a foreign correspondent for *The Christian Science Monitor* (Boston, Mass.) and contributor to French television. He recently completed a PhD in philosophy at University College Dublin.

Jane Weston Vauclair is a Paris-based researcher, university teacher and translator. Her work has notably examined the satirical output of the French satirical newspaper *Charlie Hebdo* and its forerunner *Hara-Kiri* in its theory, practice and subsequent mythologisation. Her work in the area has been published in French and English.

Preface

What can, or more accurately cannot, be said within a British university nowadays has become a major talking point. Student politics, once something people left behind upon graduation, is now the daily fare of national, and even international, news coverage. Terms like 'microaggression', 'trigger warning', and 'safe space', virtually unheard of a decade ago, have entered mainstream vocabulary.

Campus bans on everything from tabloid newspapers and fancy dress costumes to comedians and pop songs have been enforced by a vocal minority of censorious students. Those sufficiently foolhardy to attempt to speak at a university may find themselves 'no platformed'. In the past few months, Germaine Greer, Maryam Namazie and Julie Bindel have become just the most high-profile of those to have found themselves the subject of petitions to stop them speaking.

Censorious students are often looked on askance by an older, if not wiser, generation. Everyone, it seems, has a view as to whether or not the statue of the imperialist Cecil Rhodes must fall from its plinth outside Oriel College, Oxford. When Louise Richardson became the first female Vice Chancellor of Oxford University she made headline news for her defence of universities as places where all ideas can be freely debated.

Yet the comments made by Richardson, and later Chris Patten, were newsworthy because so few people from within the academy itself have the nerve to tackle censorious students head on. Some no doubt agree with the students' demands and espoused political causes; others see student politics as simply none of their business. However, the beliefs that underpin much student censorship – that words and images can inflict emotional violence and that some people, particularly those not traditionally represented within universities, are uniquely vulnerable to this oppressive psychic harm – find their origin within many strands of contemporary academic thought.

Explicit discussions about academic freedom among colleagues and in the higher education press are rare. For many working within universities there are simply more immediate concerns. The academic labour market is increasingly precarious and dependent upon a reserve pool of scholars employed on a temporary basis. Those who do enjoy the security of permanent employment still find themselves striving to meet the demands of funding bodies, research councils, peer reviewers, Research Excellence Framework (REF) panels and promotion committees, all the while teaching to produce satisfied student customers who can adequately demonstrate having met predetermined learning outcomes. Testing the limits of academic freedom and challenging a consensus may appear to be a luxury few can afford.

When the issue of academic freedom does arise it is often considered quite separately from current debates about student politics. This can make it seem as if scholars exist in a rarefied atmosphere away from the petty squabbles of student life. It is often only threats to academic freedom that emerge from heavy handed institutional managers or national government policies that warrant public condemnation.

Scholars are entirely right to draw attention to the detrimental consequences for academic freedom of the government's framework for tackling terrorism and the radicalisation of young people in schools and universities known as the Prevent Duty ('Prevent' or 'the Duty' as shorthand). The demand to monitor students and external speakers with ever more vigilance is not only entirely counterproductive to challenging radicalism, it also risks turning universities into agents, rather than critics, of the state. However, badly needed opposition to Prevent would be on a firmer footing if many scholars had not so readily and uncritically positioned themselves as supporters of state intervention not just into higher education but into many other areas of social life.

Critics of the Prevent Duty too often ignore the extent to which academic freedom has already been relinquished to myriad institutional pressures and has withered away through lack of exercise. Any last ditch attempt to resuscitate it solely through a campaign against Prevent is being fought with hands tied.

A focus on the requirements of the Prevent Duty ignores the less obvious but therefore more insidious restrictions on academic freedom that emerge from within universities from students, institutional expectations and a desire not to cause offence. It ignores the fact that many scholars choose to conform to a dominant disciplinary consensus rather than push the boundaries of what can and cannot be said. Self-censorship can become routine. For many, academic freedom is only an issue for particular individuals, specifically those who speak out of turn in a way that may be interpreted as critical of their own institution. The easier option is to conform to institutional, disciplinary and national demands and never to venture into territory considered controversial. Unfortunately, this means that academic freedom is rarely exercised and lies dormant as a set of principles. The higher education sector as a whole is in danger of losing any sense of what academic freedom means and why it matters not just to individuals but to the pursuit and transmission of knowledge.

For academic freedom to be more than just rhetoric it must be exercised. This requires scholars to have something interesting, perhaps even controversial, to say as well as the tenacity to say it. We are grateful to the contributors to this volume for being just such people. They have been bold enough to stick their heads above the parapet and ignore the admonishment that 'you can't say that'. They have addressed head on some of the key issues shaping the higher education sector today. Our hope is that this volume will prompt a broader debate about the state of academic freedom and its central importance to universities.

Joanna Williams

Why Academic Freedom Matters

Joanna Williams

The contributors to this volume range from doctoral students just embarking upon academic careers to professors with many years of experience working within higher education. They all think academic freedom matters.

Today's universities are driven by the demands of fee-paying student customers who expect satisfaction from their student experience and managers who expect obedience to the bureaucratic demands of the Research Excellence Framework (REF) and its latest off-shoot, the Teaching Excellence Framework (TEF). In this rapidly changing higher education landscape, the belief that, at some level, academic freedom matters, represents an important continuity with the past. This historical tie, even if its existence is only rhetorical, makes possible an evaluation of change. The confidence of those within universities to test and to defend academic freedom reveals much about their status within higher education institutions. Likewise, the changing arguments made in defence of academic freedom and the particular issues that are taken up in its name offer insight into the role and purpose of scholars and scholarship.

As Cheryl Hudson and Alan Ryan explore, the American Association of University Professors published its *Declaration of Principles of Academic Freedom and Academic Tenure* a century ago. In the UK, however, more generous state subsidies and the enmeshing of the professoriate within the political establishment meant few such formal statements were deemed necessary. It was only with the gradual unravelling of the post-Second World War political and economic consensus that academic freedom really became a matter for explicit discussion within universities and the public sphere more broadly.

In 1966, Lord Robbins, as President of the British Academy, gave a lecture in which he declared:

> The demand for academic freedom in institutions of higher education is not the same as the demand for freedom of thought and speech in general: it goes considerably beyond that principle. It is not merely a demand that the academic, in his capacity as a citizen, shall be free to think and speak as he likes; it is a demand that, in his employment as an academic, he shall have certain freedoms not necessarily involved in ordinary contractual relations and that the institutions in which he works shall likewise enjoy certain rights of independent initiative not necessarily granted to other institutions which are part of the state system. (Robbins, 1966, p. 48)

The confidence with which Robbins claimed that academic freedom goes 'considerably beyond' freedom of speech is sadly lacking today. Yet, even as he made such a bold declaration, Robbins also sounded a warning:

> At the present day there are some to whom the concept of academic freedom, so far from being an

2

ideal to be supported, is something which should definitely be opposed. The belief that academic life should conform to central regulations and disciplines is not something which is only to be found east of the Iron Curtain. (1966, p. 58)

This challenge to a culture of managerialism within higher education will no doubt resonate with many in academia today. However, Robbins also outlined why academic freedom was so vulnerable to bureaucratic challenge. In a statement that has proved to be sadly prophetic, Robbins argues academic freedom is most easily threatened when, 'the search for truth and values is subordinated to the exigencies of particular ideologies' (1966, p. 46).

Clearly, as Philip Cunliffe suggests, there has never been a 'golden age' of academic freedom. In different economic and political eras, different threats to academic freedom have prevailed. As the chapters in this book demonstrate, the threats to academic freedom today are as wide ranging and the arguments mounted in its defence are as various as they have ever been.

The erosion of institutional autonomy

Despite widespread fears over the impact of a rampant free-market 'neo-liberalism' upon higher education, a significant threat to academic freedom today comes from attempts made by government ministers to regulate the sector in order to meet political, social and economic objectives. Over recent decades, the erosion of institutional autonomy has occurred in conjunction with the withdrawal of directly-allocated state funding. Such regulation, as Tara McCormack and Rania Hafez indicate, poses its most explicit challenge to academic freedom with anti-terrorism legislation. The Counter-Terrorism and Security Act 2015 led to the implementation of the Prevent Duty designed to tackle the perceived threats to UK security posed by religious extremism and radicalisation on campus.

Prevent puts the onus on universities to vet external speakers and bar anyone who may be intent upon radicalising students. Often academics are themselves external speakers and are thereby recruited into monitoring and checking on each other. At the same time, lecturers are also expected to monitor the attendance and behaviour of the students they come into contact with and report to the authorities any international students on visas who fail to attend or students who are present but act 'suspiciously'. The story of the Staffordshire student who was investigated after being spotted reading a book on terrorism in the university library (Ramesh and Halliday, 24/09/15) is indicative of how surveillance changes the relationship between academics and students. This is detrimental to the trust necessary for learning and teaching.

Recent government policies also contribute to the erosion of academic freedom in less explicit ways. Repeated attempts have been made to increase the competitiveness of the nation's higher education sector and to make universities more responsive to external demands from the state or from industry. This has led to shifts in the sector's funding away from 'block grants' based primarily on student numbers towards more market driven approaches intended to promote competition for fee-paying customers and research income. As Anthony J. Stanonis shows, the REF, with its target-obsessed measurement of outputs and impact, has brought into existence a cadre of administrators and academics recruited to strategise about the most effective route to institutional success. This involves encouraging the submission of papers to an increasingly narrow selection of journals and 'gaming the system' to enhance the likelihood of publication by selecting topics and referring to papers with an appeal to the editorial stance of the journal. The exercise of academic freedom is suppressed by the drive to ensure conformity to the demands of the all-consuming REF.

At the same time, the funding of teaching in higher education has shifted on to students as individual customers of a particular institution. This has contributed towards a relentless focus on student satisfaction with academics expected to demonstrate their responsiveness to the demands of the student voice. As the status of students within the university is elevated, the capacity for lecturers to teach and assess what and how they choose to do so is compromised. Again, an army of managers and administrators, many of them fellow academics, is on hand to ensure institutional success in satisfaction league tables. As a result, teaching has become commoditised into learning outcomes that can be known in advance and allocated credits and contact hours which can be publicly advertised in student charters and key information sets. The freedom of academics to follow an interesting line of argument to its logical conclusion, or to be idiosyncratic and spontaneous in teaching or assessment methods, has suffered as a result.

Students as censors

The desire of universities and some lecturers to appease rather than challenge students is not just driven by changes to government legislation. As Kathryn Ecclestone and Jenny Jarvie indicate, there is also a growing perception, often among more politically radical academics, that students are vulnerable. This leads to a growing demand to turn lecture theatre and campus into a safe space. Course content may come with 'trigger warnings', advance notification if potentially distressing topics are likely to be covered, and lecturers tend to think carefully before including material likely to upset the sensibilities of some students on the curriculum. Academics may begin to self-censor so as not to cause offence.

When academics support the perception of students as vulnerable they are not then in a position to challenge demands for censorship, or attacks on academic freedom, that arise from students themselves. There have been high-profile cases of students' unions banning from campus anything from newspapers, songs, greetings cards and hats to fancy dress costumes, on the grounds that they objectify women, promote rape culture or demonstrate cultural appropriation. This new form of campus censorship extends into re-writing history with the demand for statues, such as that of Cecil Rhodes at Oriel College, Oxford, to be removed if the ideology of the person represented does not meet the political standards of the students of today (Ezaz, 30/10/15).

Such campus censorship often hits the headlines when high-profile speakers are 'no platformed', or in other words, banned from speaking on campus. James Heartfield explores how, in October 2015, the feminist philosopher and intellectual Germaine Greer made the news when students at the University of Cardiff launched a petition to stop her giving a lecture on the subject of 'Women and Power'. Students were offended by the prospect of Greer's presence on campus because of opinions about transgenderism she had expressed many years previously. Greer had not been planning to talk about this particular issue in her Cardiff lecture. Few academics publicly defended Greer's reputation or her right to accept an invitation to speak in a university. Her freedom to talk about a topic she had spent her life researching was at risk of being curtailed and hardly anyone made the case that this was an attack on academic freedom.

The ongoing campaigns that have emerged in the US and the UK against ideas that are labelled as offensive by a vocal minority of students close down debate and discussion on campus. They perpetuate the notion that words can wound and that vulnerable students need to be protected from ideas, or knowledge, they consider distasteful rather than university being the best place in society to discuss, question and challenge everything in the interests of promoting understanding and the pursuit of knowledge. The role of the academic risks becoming less concerned with prompting debate or pushing the boundaries of knowledge into new areas and more to do with shielding students from ideas that may upset them. When universities are happy to put ideas beyond discussion their mission is no longer education.

In general, academia poses little challenge to censorship that emanates from within the student body. Academics who consider students to be vulnerable, and that words and ideas can endanger an already fragile sense of self, often actively support bans (see for example Laurie, 29/10/15). Alternatively, some lecturers will argue that students have a right to no platform speakers and that doing so is actually an expression of their free speech (see for example Cutterham, 03/12/15). Others simply consider it none of their business. The contorted logic by which censorship comes to be considered a demonstration of free speech suggests book burning is similarly an example of free expression. It is an undemocratic and elitist means of by-passing debate in order to prevent certain views from being heard. The argument that students have a right to decide who can and cannot speak on campus is symptomatic of the privileging of the student voice on campus. This has been paralleled by a decline in the status and influence of academics at an institutional level. Nonetheless, it is a cowardly abdication of responsibility. Academics should be developing in students an intellectual robustness and an ability to argue against ideas they find unpleasant rather than tacitly supporting the censorship of challenging views.

Academics as censors

Some scholars are reluctant to criticise student censors because they have political sympathy with the causes the students espouse. They consider that the specific principles, be they pro-feminist, pro-transgender, anti-Israeli, or anti-sexist, trump the more fundamental demand for academic freedom. Academics unable to defend the significance of any particular disciplinary-specific body of knowledge, or the relationship between knowledge and truth, have reached a consensus that all knowledge is subjective, partial and political. To this end, they reject the need for academic freedom as a means of allowing the advance of knowledge through competing contestable truth claims. In its place comes the promotion of skills and values. If all knowledge is political then knowledge that supports the rights of historically disadvantaged or minority groups is more morally virtuous than knowledge that appears to defend those in more privileged positions. Students pick up on this message in the lecture theatre and enact it in practice.

When academics tacitly support student censors, they find that the terrain to participate in debate is closed down for them too. As Jane Weston Vauclair and Jason Walsh show, the logic of arguing that some debates are too dangerous to be held on campus means that not only students are prevented from taking part in debates but academics are too. They either find themselves 'no platformed' or that the debates they had wanted to participate in are cancelled.

Academics who think that political principles trump academic freedom end up censoring each other. One example of this can be seen in scholarly debates around the issue of rape. The widely held assumption that 'rape myths' are prevalent and dangerous is used to close down debate as all discussion can be said to perpetrate such myths and therefore contribute to a climate whereby women feel responsible for their own rape and do not report crimes (see Reece, 2016 and Williams, 2016).

In October 2013 Helen Reece, a Reader in Law at the London School of Economics spoke at a public event entitled *Is Rape Different?* She argued that the prevalence of rape myths is overstated and that some attitudes described as myths actually reflect reality. A group of feminist critical lawyers based at the University of Kent published a response to the debate which acted as a petition calling for the LSE to 'ensure that the ideas disseminated [at the debate] do not feed dangerous stereotypes about women being responsible for the sexual violence perpetrated against them' (Editors, 2013). This was a call from one group of academics to restrict the freedom of a fellow academic to participate in a debate on the assumption that a free discussion of the issue of rape, particularly one that involves members of the public, is somehow dangerous. We see that, however well-intentioned, the threat to academic freedom in this instance comes not from national government, university managers or students but from fellow scholars.

A further argument, again made by academics seeking to restrict discussion of rape more broadly and the publicity around the LSE debate in particular, was that the freedom afforded to a few individuals in positions of power (academics) served to undermine the more general free speech rights of rape survivors who perhaps lacked the confidence or security to discuss their situation openly. The argument was made that only by restricting dominant opposing voices could the free speech of the more vulnerable hope to be safeguarded. However, as soon as speech rights are set in opposition to one another in this way then an individual or a group is left responsible for deciding who gets to speak based, presumably, on the proposed content of the arguments or the identity of the speaker. As academics are, by definition, most often the ones in powerful positions when discussing issues with the public – and for a good reason, they have done the research in this area – any attempt to distribute speech rights based on power is a threat to academic freedom.

Ultimately, following the logic of this argument, free speech for some becomes free speech for no one as all are expected to comply with the moral framework determined by a 'dictatorship of the virtuous' (Strossen, 2000). In academia, just as in society at large, which voices get heard has never been determined on the basis of the moral status of the speaker or the virtue of the subject matter. While this may be unfair, and is certainly not always nice, it is only through a clash of competing views that new ideas can challenge and, based on the validity of the arguments proposed, perhaps even supersede previously held orthodoxies. For this reason, it is always in the interests of underrepresented groups and minority views for there to be more free speech rather than less.

The tendency for academics to police themselves and each other means that formal restrictions on academic freedom, although problematic, are actually rarely needed. One danger is that self-censorship becomes a routine part of academic life. New lecturers quickly learn how to avoid upsetting the student-customers who pay their wages and how to please the peer-reviewers who will green-light their work for publication and them for promotion. They learn how to comply with all manner of speech codes, safe space and anti-harassment policies. Routine self-censorship not only does away with the need for too many overt restrictions on academic freedom, it also reinforces an intolerance of dissent.

In June 2015, Nobel Prize winning biochemist Tim Hunt was publicly criticised by fellow scientists and academics following remarks he made about the 'problem' of women in laboratories. That he is married to leading immunologist Mary Collins and has a track record of supporting and advancing women's careers in science did not prevent a public outcry over the supposedly damaging impact of his unguarded comment. From social media to mainstream newspapers Hunt's remarks were dissected and he was condemned for being an old white man with views that were a relic of a bygone era and needed to be purged from academia. When Hunt's resignation from his honorary position at University College London was accepted, rather than defending his right to free speech, a number of prominent academics expressed satisfaction that he had demonstrably been punished for his crime of sexist speech (Bishop, 16/07/15). As a result of being called out for using the wrong words, Hunt lost his job and his reputation. He is now better known for being sexist than making scientific breakthroughs in the treatment of cancer. Tim Hunt's case is illustrative of how certain views come to dominate higher education. New academics quickly become aware of this consensus and learn that their lives are easier, and their careers progress more smoothly, if they keep quiet and do not say anything controversial.

The empty rhetoric of academic freedom

Today, some scholars explicitly criticise the concept of academic freedom. It stands accused of propagating a liberal view of the scholar as an autonomous individual, travelling free from experiences of prejudice and unencumbered by practical and emotional commitments through a politically neutral intellectual terrain. Academic freedom is criticised for reinforcing the right to a platform for those who are already in dominant positions and doing nothing to challenge the structural inequalities that make it more difficult for less powerful groups to have their voices heard. Omar Barghouti, a founding committee member of the 'Palestinian Campaign for the Academic and Cultural Boycott of Israel' suggests, 'academic freedom is sometimes in conflict with basic human rights' and concludes, 'when such conflicts occur it must be that basic human rights are the more important good to defend' (in Butler, 2006 p. 9). The American literary theorist and legal scholar Stanley Fish has caricatured this argument as meaning, 'while academic freedom is usually a good thing, when basic questions of justice are in play, it must give way' (Fish, 28/10/13).

Alongside such criticisms of academic freedom sit attempts to redefine what the concept means. With its epistemological basis undermined, the rhetoric of academic freedom is increasingly attached to principles that run counter to free speech and free expression (see Williams, 2016). Academic freedom is reimagined as a matter of social justice and called upon to silence supposedly powerful groups while allowing the voices of previously underrepresented groups to be heard.

Attempts to redefine academic freedom as a matter of justice arise most clearly in campaigns to boycott Israeli universities. Proponents of Boycott, Divestment and Sanctions (BDS) argue that Israeli universities receive government funding in return for playing a cultural role propagandising on behalf of a state that engages in systematic acts of oppression against Palestinians. They claim that interaction with the rest of the world legitimises and politically-neutralises Israeli universities and, by default, the nation state. Attempts to defend the academic freedom of Israeli scholars are frequently rejected outright with the claim that because the Israeli state prevents Palestinian professors and students from attending universities, travelling to conferences, and engaging in scholarship, then Israeli academics have no right to academic freedom themselves.

BDS proponents argue that restricting the academic freedom of Israeli scholars as a result of political and military decisions, that most did not instigate and many may not actually support, is justified when seen in comparison to the scale of human rights abuses conducted against the Palestinians. However, imposing constraints on Israeli academics as a punishment for the sins of the nation introduces political conditions upon academic freedom. What should be, within the academy at least, a universal right to further the pursuit of knowledge, comes to be defined politically and selectively, applicable only to those who share the 'correct' views or live in the 'correct' part of the world. Butler's desire for 'a more inclusive version of the doctrine across national borders and along egalitarian lines' (2006, p. 10) uses equality and inclusivity to argue for some speech to be silenced so the voices of others can be heard.

The introduction of political judgement negates the concept of academic freedom. As Fish indicates, it brings about a complete reversal in the definition of academic freedom, 'from a doctrine insulating the academy from politics into a doctrine that demands of academics blatantly political actions' (28/10/13). BDS supporters ask fellow academics to make judgements about who gets to speak, whose research gets published, and what students are taught, not on the basis of what is considered most useful in advancing knowledge and arriving closer to a (still contestable) truth but on the national identity of the speakers and the political views they espouse. Not only is this antithetical to the pursuit of knowledge it is also inherently undemocratic. Questions as to whose view of justice should prevail and which views are unacceptable are rarely raised when a prevailing political consensus is assumed.

Why academic freedom matters

A fundamental tenet of academic freedom is that all truth claims are contestable and nothing should be beyond question. It is only correct that this questioning is turned on the principle of academic freedom and that scholars consider the assumptions inherent within the concept itself. The notion of academic freedom that emerged within the academy over a century ago was built upon a particular view of scholarship that assumed objectivity and political neutrality in the knowledge pursued. It is always useful to shine a light on these assumptions and question whether knowledge is, or indeed ever can be, objective in its truth claims. Likewise, it is important to question whether the traditional notion of academic freedom supports a particular political perspective and prevents other views from being heard.

Those who argue for academic justice play a useful role in pointing out that the assumed objectivity of scholarship inherent in the concept of academic freedom can mask work that is not politically neutral but instead confirms existing power relations. However, rather than striving for more objective research, proponents of academic justice seek instead to make explicit the political values that underpin scholarship. This paves the way for academic work to be judged not on the basis of its intellectual contribution to the pursuit of knowledge but according to the sympathy or otherwise for the position espoused.

The aim to be more critical, better to challenge existing norms and to arrive at superior understanding, is to be welcomed. Indeed, it must drive academic work and can best be achieved by questioning the assumptions that underpin what counts as scholarship. However, arguing for academic justice is not the same as arguing for better, more objective knowledge that brings us closer to truth. It is a call on scholars to abandon objectivity altogether in favour of taking a political position that has been pre-determined by others. The assumption of objectivity inherent in academic freedom was not always met and did indeed provide a veneer of neutrality for work that was political. However, challenging this by abandoning objectivity and establishing a political position not only prevents academics from aspiring towards contestable truth claims, it enforces consensus and political conformity on academic work that curtails questioning and criticality from the outset.

Academic freedom matters because it allows for the unrestricted pursuit and passing on of knowledge. Knowledge advances through the freedom to provoke, cause offence and upset the status quo. There is simply no point in higher education without academic freedom. Universities risk returning to being medieval institutions, only instead of paying homage to the church they now worship at the altar of 'progressive' opinion.

To reinvigorate academic freedom, scholars need to recognise threats to academic freedom for what they really are and not allow academic freedom to be redefined as restricting free speech. The prevention of offence must not be placed above the right to debate. The pursuit of knowledge, rather than the promotion of values, skills or personal behaviour must lie at the heart of the university. This requires a concept of knowledge that is neither fixed for all time nor reducible to ideology. It is the social composition of knowledge – collective individual reason tested out in the marketplace of ideas – that gives it the status of truth albeit a truth that remains permanently contestable. Academics need to treat students and members of the public alike as capable, intelligent, rational and autonomous individuals, capable of engaging in reasoned debate. They need to encourage the free exchange of ideas rather than looking to close down debates. Most importantly of all, academic freedom only survives through being continually exercised in the classroom, in scholarly journals and in the public square. If not exercised, academic freedom becomes reduced to rhetoric or dead dogma. It is up to scholars who care about academic freedom to make sure this does not happen.

References

Bishop, D. (2015) 'The trouble with jokes about girls' in *Times Higher Education* (16/07/15). Available at: https://www.times highereducation.com/opinion/the-trouble-with-jokes-about-girls (accessed 04/12/15).

Butler, J. (2006) 'Israel/Palestine and the Paradoxes of Academic Freedom' in *Radical Philosophy* (135) pp. 8–17.

Cutterham, T. (2015) 'Today's students are anything but coddled' in *Times Higher Education* (03/12/15). Available at: https://www. timeshighereducation.com/features/todays-students-are-anything-but-coddled (accessed 04/12/15).

Ramesh, R. and Halliday, J. (2015) 'Student accused of being a terrorist for reading a book on terrorism' in *The Guardian* (24/09/15). Available at: http://www.theguardian.com/education/2015/sep/24/student-accused-being-terrorist-reading-book-terrorism?CMP=share_btn_tw (accessed 04/12/15).

Editors. (2013) 'Editorial: A Response to the LSE event "Is Rape Different?"' in *Feminists@Law*, 3 (2). Available at: http://journals.kent.ac.uk/index.php/feministsatlaw/article/view/80/21 2 (accessed 30/03/16).

Ezaz, C. (2015) 'Rhodes remains a symbol of racism in Oxford' in *The Oxford Student* (30/10/15). Available at: http://oxfordstudent.com/2015/10/30/rhodes-remains-a-symbol-of-racism-in-oxford/ (accessed 04/12/15).

Fish, S. (2013) 'Academic Freedom Against Itself: Boycotting Israeli Universities' in *The New York Times*, (28/10/13). Available at: http://opinionator.blogs.nytimes.com/2013/10/28/academic-freedom-against-itself-boycotting-israeli-universities/ (accessed 25/01/15).

Laurie, T. (2015) 'Against Freedom of Speech in Higher Education: A Response to Germaine Greer' in *NewMatilda.com* (29/10/15). Available at: https://newmatilda.com/2015/10/29/against-freedom-of-speech-in-higher-education-a-response-to-germaine-gre er/ (accessed 04/12/15).

Reece, H. (2013) 'Rape Myths: Is Elite Opinion Right and Popular Opinion Wrong?' in *Oxford Journal of Legal Studies*, 33 (3) pp. 445–473.

Robbins, L. (1966) 'Of Academic Freedom' in *Higher Education Quarterly*, (20) pp. 420–435.

Williams, J. (2016) *Academic Freedom in an Age of Conformity, Confronting the Fear of Knowledge.* London: Palgrave Macmillan.

A Century of Academic Freedom

Cheryl Hudson

Once appointed, the scholar has professional functions to perform in which the appointing authorities have neither competency nor moral right to intervene. The responsibility of the university teacher is primarily to the public itself, and to the judgment of his own profession.

- American Association of University Professors, 1915

The interplay between historical context and abstract principle animates the story of academic freedom in the century since the American Association of University Professors' (AAUP) initial *Declaration of Principles on Academic Freedom and Academic Tenure*. This declaration, issued in 1915 and updated in 1940, defined the rationale for academic freedom in the modern era. Although the UK had no comparable formal statement, in response to recent threats to free academic enquiry in the UK, the University and College Union (UCU) issued a declaration of academic freedom loosely modelled on the AAUP *Declaration* in 2009.

The context of the 1915 *Declaration* and the principles it sets down demand interrogation and explanation in its centennial year (it was adopted by its membership in 1916), as pressing questions continue to emerge about why academic thought, speech and practice require special protection over and above that granted other forms of thought, speech and practice. What is the relationship between the context of their framing and the principles themselves? Do the 'principles' of academic freedom as defined by the AAUP in fact simply serve as a smoke-screen for the furtherance of narrow professional interest? Or do they undermine the rights of students and the public not to be misled, distracted or offended by irresponsible, elitist or prejudiced academics? Perhaps they serve only as a shield for the pursuance of radical political goals unrelated to disinterested, objective scholarship? More pressingly, are the principles of academic freedom no longer relevant in the age of Je Suis Charlie tolerance in Europe or, in the American context, where a strong democratic tradition of free speech is unencumbered by elitist claims to knowledge and power? Many of these criticisms and claims existed at the AAUP's founding and remain current and active one hundred years on.

Before testing the principles of academic freedom in the context of contemporary Britain, as the contributors to this volume do in various ways, it is worth establishing how the AAUP's 1915 *Declaration* defined those principles and asking how principled the organisation was in its own defence of academic freedom. Here, I will sketch the historical context in which the principles emerged and address whether, given the many contingencies at play, academic freedom should be taken seriously as a universal standard. I will ask whether the particular context of the first articulation of academic freedom undermines it as a claim that can profitably be applied in diverse settings, including that of twenty-first century Britain.

The founding principles

Although most of the founding members of the AAUP thought infringements on academic freedom were not a significant problem because they occurred only intermittently, it is notable that the first and defining action of the new association was to declare academic freedom and tenure essential to the professional mission and status of university scholars.

The 1915 *Declaration* claimed three important freedoms: of research and enquiry; of teaching; and of speech and action outside of the University. The AAUP identified the boards of trustees that governed most US universities as the central threat to scholarly autonomy but the Association undertook to protect these freedoms from encroachment or restriction from any quarter. It would work to allow academic research, teaching and public engagement to continue free from religious, political or commercial impediments as well as interference from universities and the state. It pledged too to prevent academic appointments from becoming just another cog in the well-greased wheels of city or state political machines or distributed as a reward of political spoils. Indeed, freedom and tenure are strongly linked within the AAUP's *Declaration*. It requires that only disinterested scholars and not those with political, or any other ulterior motivations, perform the gatekeeping of the profession – that is, the recruitment, hiring and promotion of its members. Objectivity was a key value in the operationalisation of professionalism among university professors.

The nature of the academic calling informed the *Declaration*: the AAUP thought it important to have men of character and talent in the profession. (The number of female lecturers remained small for many reasons, none having to do with academic freedom. Indeed, in 1921, the AAUP conducted one of the first surveys of the status of women in academia and found that of the 100 co-educational institutions surveyed, 27 had no women on faculty at all. Among those that did, women held only four per cent of professorial positions.) Its concern with gender imbalance reflected the AAUP's determination that beyond the pursuit of knowledge in their field, there must be no cause for suspicion of academics' motivations. Protecting the freedom of academics from the demands of both public opinion and from the diktat of university management was judged essential to protecting the status of the academic calling. In other words, a lack of freedom would undermine all claims to status as impartial experts across the profession, for both outspoken and conformist academics alike. If academic enquiry was fettered for one, it was rendered suspect for all.

The *Declaration* also stated that academics must be recognised as appointees rather than employees. That is, professors must have the same freedoms of thought, speech and action as that exercised by a federal judge. The distinction between employee and appointee was an important one since regular first amendment speech carries protection from censorship by the state. Academic freedom, on the other hand, carries protection from censure by an employer. In order to justify this novel form of freedom in 1915, the AAUP asserted professional expertise as the rationale for enlarging the professoriate's sphere of unregulated action. Interference or censure by either an employer or the state not only damaged professional status but also undermined the disinterested status of all research and teaching conducted in the university. It was therefore in the interest of both employer and employee to ring-fence academic activities from non-scholarly influence. It was also, the AAUP claimed, in the interest of the general good despite placing academic activities beyond the reach of democratic accountability (federal justices being, incidentally, the only level of judge to be appointed rather than elected).

Thus, to perform any academic role, either as a researcher with the aim of advancing knowledge, a teacher imparting knowledge to students and encouraging them to think critically, or as an impartial expert whose skills might be employed for the public good, a scholar must be, and must be seen to be, free to follow any line of enquiry. The AAUP deemed the autonomy to question, interrogate and scrutinise all aspects of a subject in any manner imaginable essential to ensure that a professor's integrity and disinterestedness remained unquestioned. Of course, the freedoms protected belonged to teachers but not to students, indeed only to tenured academics of ten years standing. More junior members of the profession were not protected since they were barred from AAUP membership. But underlying the special, privileged claim to freedom in pursuit of knowledge was a noble regard for the special status of objective knowledge.

The historical context

The historical conditions under which the AAUP emerged and formulated the principles of academic freedom are important for understanding the organisation's motives. There are two alternative narratives that seek to explain them. On the one hand, liberal commentators, including the AAUP itself, claim that the organisation arose in response to a series of grave threats to academic freedom to which the AAUP provided a robust collective defence. On the other hand, less sympathetic observers suggest that anxious professional academics sought to ring fence their privileged access to expertise and social status in the face of an unwieldy, unpredictable democratic upsurge. There are insights in and limitations to both approaches.

The large-scale industrialisation and urbanisation that took place in the US at the turn of the twentieth century produced dramatic social upheaval on many fronts. Americans experienced the onslaught of modernity, with the many associated shifts in social norms and cultural values further exaggerated by the impact of scientific ideas, fostered by the new research universities. In no small measure, scientific authority replaced religious authority and, in urban centres at least, the power and influence of traditional institutions, notably of church and family, began to fade. Widening social divisions and the expression of political interests in collective ways shook confidence in liberal individualism. To many observers, society seemed split in two: between the 'masses' and the 'classes' with capital conglomerations and manufacturers' associations on one side and national trade unions emerging on the other. In the midst of all this social turbulence and uncertainty, the middle classes pushed back against their relative marginalisation, feeling unsettled but also very curious. Among them, a new class of college professors sought to assert their own claim to authority and concomitant social status. The newly founded research universities began to investigate the world under these novel conditions and to generate technical know-how to manage them. Robert Wiebe's classic study of the progressive 'search for order', describes how the professionalisation of middle class occupations represented the forging of a new social elite for the modern age (Wiebe, 1980). While capital and labour slugged it out, the new bureaucratic elite remade the political culture. In the midst of growing unionisation, professional groups also recognised collective action as a necessary mode for the negotiation of interest and for the protection of status.

In the midst of this social turmoil, a number of academics lost their jobs. The case that the AAUP points to as the catalyst to its own creation is that of Stanford University sociologist Edward A. Ross. Mrs Leland Stanford, widow of the railway magnate and founder and sole benefactor of Stanford University, ostensibly had Ross fired for racism directed at Asian immigrants. The reality was, in fact, more complicated. While Ross was indeed an advocate of eugenicist policies, he had also been a fierce and outspoken critic of political corruption especially the corruption endemic in the relationship between the Republican Party and the railroads. Leland Stanford had been a Republican governor of California as well as a director of the Central Pacific Railroad, which had been involved in building the first transcontinental railroad in the United States. As a politician Stanford had himself made many racist public statements. In 1862, for example, he outlined to the state legislature his determination to defend the superior white race against the degradations of the Chinese. Yet, as a railroad investor he came to depend on Asian, especially Chinese, labour and so tempered his opposition to immigration. His widow's firing of Ross for his outspoken comments was an attack on academic freedom in defence of the Stanfords' political and business interests. Several other professors at Stanford resigned in protest.

The Ross case has gained something of a retrospective 'founding myth' status for the AAUP but this is inaccurate in two details. First, it was not the first prominent academic freedom case. That honour is better awarded to University of Chicago economist Edward Bemis, who had been fired from his position for speaking out on behalf of railroad workers and strikers of Debs's American Railway Union during the 1894 Pullman Strike. The first president of the AAUP, philosopher John Dewey, was a colleague of Bemis's at Chicago but Dewey, like all of Bemis's colleagues, remained silent over his treatment. Dewey's biographer notes that 'there was no comment in his letters or his published writings on the dismissal of the economist Edward Bemis' in 1894. Only after 1915 was Dewey 'brave enough in sticking up for academic liberty' (Ryan, 1995, pp. 168–69).

Second, it is hard to see how either Bemis's or Ross's case, occurring in 1894 and 1900 respectively, were direct catalysts for the founding of the AAUP so many years later. The immediate context and spur to action, in 1915, was the outbreak of war. Although the US did not enter the Great War until 1917, the political climate was becoming more brittle, conformist and nationalistic. Probably the most celebrated academic freedom case was that of Scott Nearing – like Bemis, a radical economist – who was employed at the University of Pennsylvania's Wharton Business School. Nearing's criticisms of child labour and other exploitative features of industrial capitalism had irritated the trustees for some time but when he questioned corporate motivations for supporting American preparedness for war in 1915, the administration terminated his contract, acting against the recommendation of his department, a Wharton School reappointments committee and the School's dean. His colleagues, conscious of the implicit threat to their own autonomy, responded swiftly.

While university professors were leery of taking sides in the great class battles of their time, their liberal proclivities encouraged them to resist state- or employer- enforced conformity. The AAUP rallied to support Nearing and numerous other academics who lost their jobs for adopting an anti-war position during the First World War. His case flagged up to academics of all political stripes how essential academic freedom was to the perception of their own independence from the college trustees or president. As one Wharton School professor noted, 'the moment Nearing went, any conservative statement became but the spoken word of a "kept" professor' (Whitfield, 1974, p. 36). The firing from Columbia in 1917 of psychologist James Cattell and literary scholar Henry Dana for supporting the exemption of conscientious objectors from conscription triggered a strong reaction from their colleagues. Historians Charles Beard and James Harvey Robinson resigned and went on to found the New School for Social Research with other likeminded progressives, including philosopher John Dewey, the first president of the AAUP.

Many of the academics losing their jobs in the early years of the century were social scientists keenly interested in the social and economic turmoil and cultural disruptions of the times. University administrations interpreted their tendency to advocate for particular social justice causes as an abrogation of their responsibility to scientific objectivity. Their dismissal was thus justified; the University of Chicago's President Harper argued that Bemis had forgotten that 'to serve the University we must employ scientific methods and do scientific work' and that Bemis had allowed his personal views to confound that objective (Novick, 1988, p. 68). The AAUP conceived of itself as a calming, steady hand. It would act as the objective and disinterested observer, calm social passions and institute scholarship – scientific, social scientific and humanistic – as the new source of social authority to replace those that modernity had disrupted. Thus, both those who defended and those who sought to limit academic freedom in the early twentieth century acted in the name of objectivity. Both Mrs Stanford and E.A. Ross had asserted their own interest in the pursuit of objective truth.

The context within which academic freedom emerged as a principle, then, neither undermines nor elevates those principles in the ways that commentators suggest. The AAUP responded to two social trends intensifying throughout the Western world. First, it was part of a broad professionalisation project and thereby sought to define and defend university professors' status and standing just as professional associations did for doctors and lawyers (Tiede, 2014). Second, it responded to the censorious climate developing during the Great War. The AAUP sought to defend its members' interests as expert professionals distinct from the masses who might pose a threat to national security. Their disciplinary expertise, as members of communities of competent enquiry, distinguished them from the common citizenry. Some founding members had less than democratic inclinations and a greater regard for protecting their professional status than defending free speech and thought. Others had loftier ideals but could only act pragmatically in consort with their fellow professionals. The research university institutionalised the difference between scientific evidence and public opinion clearly and forcefully. In modern political culture, elite experts: that is, not the 'masses' and not the 'interests', would discover social truths and transform them into evidence-based policy.

Academic freedom today

The AAUP's *Declaration of Principles* in 1915 was ultimately a pragmatic adjustment to a new social reality. It offered a partial freedom for elitist ends. However, in the twenty-first century it has become more fashionable to focus on the limitations of academic freedom rather than its benefits. Louis Menand, while recognising that academic freedom is essential to the entire enterprise of the university, suggests that it is inherently limited by the exclusivity it imposes (Menand, 1996, p. 9). Ronald Dworkin urges us to recognise that academic freedom is just one value among many and must be limited in the face of competing claims (Dworkin, 1996). Even Steven Salaita, who became something of a cause célèbre among defenders of academic freedom in 2015, does not himself support the same freedoms for Israeli scholars (Salaita, 2015). As early as the 1930s, John Dewey, the first president of AAUP, expressed frustration with the limitations of the phrase 'academic freedom', thinking it overly technical and remote: he preferred the term 'freedom of education' which conveyed a greater social connection and democratic significance (Dewey, 1936). Indeed, beneath the objections to it lies a concern that it depends upon a concept of liberal individualism, a concept that social progressives are uncomfortable with. Yet, while academic freedom might not do all the work that social progressives want it to do, it most certainly does valuable work.

The principle can and should be separated from the context in which it arose. In a twenty-first century context, we should avoid throwing the proverbial baby out with the bath water. Academic freedom emerged and was subsequently applied in a limiting context but recognising this need not undermine the underlying principle. It is more than worth considering what the principle of academic freedom continues to lay claim to. Indeed, the problems with academic freedom can only be resolved with an expansion of the freedoms it offers; certainly not by an imposition of more or increased limits arising from its new context.

In 1776, the principles of the American Declaration of Independence did not align with their historical reality. That is, the colonial context militated against its claims: Thomas Jefferson, the author of the document, heralded the equality of all men while owning slaves. Indeed, he belonged to a class of men who generally owned slaves and the political economy of the new nation was built on a foundation of slavery. For sure, the context was highly problematic but the principle of human equality appealed to an important and enduring truth. It is only a truth that could endure because new people in new contexts breathed life back into it. Almost two centuries on, Martin Luther King cashed in, as he saw it, on the promissory note written by the slave-owning, liberty-loving founders. Political principles can, and do, outlive the circumstances in which they are initially formulated and can be wielded and given new meaning and new life by future generations.

The principle of academic freedom, as outlined by the AAUP in 1915, was a good one and it is time for the scholars, teachers and researchers of the present generation to cash in on the promissory note written in the dark days of wartime censorship, job insecurity and anxious professionalisation. Academic freedom, like any freedom, is both an individual and a social good and its realm should be expanded and secured. The context has changed, undoubtedly, and as many contributors here note, many of the threats to academic freedom now come from within the academy itself. The key role of the university has also changed and the epistemological shifts that have undermined objectivity make the challenges to freedom different, but no less real.

It is worth asking whether a rigorous defence of academic freedom depends upon faith in objective knowledge and the pursuit of truth. The founders of the AAUP hoped to fence knowledge off from power but many scholars today – at least in the humanities – concur with Foucault's challenge to the distinction between knowledge and power, collapsing them into one category (Haskell, 1996, p. 48). This shift might lie at the heart of why so many contributors to this book understand the problem as belonging within the university itself. What is fairly certain is that universities must allow experts space to think about this, and other questions, with a free reign if academic life is to avoid becoming (or remaining) stifling and conformist, dominated by groupthink and platitudes.

The pursuit of knowledge is no doubt challenged by political advocacy but it is offered greater challenge – and becomes more difficult to defend – from a lapse into dull conformity. The mouthing of hackneyed truisms is more of a threat in a university setting than claims to objective truth. Or, as Russell Jacoby puts it in his humorous caricature of Stanley Fish's dismissal of objective knowledge in favour of social constructionism: 'Academics don't eat shit anymore; now they serve it, and in a pinch they don't care whose shit they serve' (22/08/13). Jacoby's serious point is that the insights of historicism, 'that everything is historical, contextual, or situated', are in danger of becoming banal dross by sheer weight of repetition in the seminar room and conference hall (22/08/13).

The contributors to this volume offer a challenge to Stanley Fish's administrative pragmatism and to the epistemological relativism he endorses by raising questions about the relationship between the context that academic freedom operates in and the principle it asserts. We collectively argue that the principle of academic freedom must be defended by reconnecting it with broader principles of liberty, even in a context of heightened security demands and/or loss of authority by the university more broadly. Indeed, it is precisely because the arguments for knowledge and truth from within the university are so weak and narrow that academic freedom can come under such sustained and successful attack as it has recently. This volume hopes to fortify the barricades on the side of those who, like Jacoby, have already begun the resistance against the degradation of the value of knowledge and for the freedom to pursue it.

Figuring out how to best defend the principle of academic freedom is an important challenge and one that Phillip Cunliffe, Alan Ryan, Dennis Hayes and James Heartfield address in the first section of the book. Alan Ryan explores the relationship between academic freedom and broader social rights and freedoms on the one hand, and individual liberties on the other. He makes a positive liberationist case for the truth function as essential to the role of the university and to any full understanding of academic freedom. Phillip Cunliffe concurs by warning against the use of negative defensive mechanisms alone in the fight for academic freedom. Rather than either viewing the past through rose-tinted glasses or battling straw men intent on stealing their freedom, Cunliffe suggests, academics must adopt an active stance in marking out their own agenda for freedom in the university. Dennis Hayes offers an institutional means through which UK academics might begin to do this in the form of 'Academics For Academic Freedom'. He argues that making a stronger connection between academic freedom and more general free speech rights must be the first step. James Heartfield raises the question of whether present day academics want or need to exercise freedom at all, trapped as they are within a conservative epistemology of identity that shuns reason.

The intellectual and institutional context within which British academics work is the subject of the second section of the book, exploring the university in the twenty-first century. Thomas Docherty explicitly compares the contexts of 1915 and 2015 through the role of proprietary institutions and expresses concern at the direction universities are taking. He argues that an increasing privatisation – especially in the atomising orientation of scholars competing for status and resources – is undermining universities' primary duty to the public. He discusses the role of disciplinarity and its inclination toward the policing and punishment of non-conformist thought and action. Rania Hafez wrestles with the increasingly uncomfortable coexistence of religious faith and secular knowledge in institutions of higher education. Academics have lost the freedom to explore all facets of the ideas and belief systems that sustain and motivate people. Anthony J. Stanonis documents the ways in which the mechanisms of the centrally coordinated Research Excellence Framework remove autonomy from researchers and fasten a conservative agenda on departments, faculties and schools.

The remaining contributions deal with the reasons why academics need freedom today and the challenges they face from both within and without the university. What Isaiah Berlin outlined as negative liberties, or 'freedom from' incursions from government remain an issue for those interested in academic freedom; but so do external demands on academics from employers, market mechanisms and the moral imperatives of public opinion. The defence of professional autonomy is an important part of the defence that both Anthony Stanonis and Tara McCormack take up in their essays. Many of the contributors to this volume allude to the government's new counter-terrorist Prevent Duty but Tara McCormack comprehensively delineates the ways that it undermines freedom and the many reasons that academics should resist its implementation.

The threats from within, or the conditions that prevent academics launching the kind of positive fight for academic freedom that Phillip Cunliffe advocates, are not straightforward. Here, contributors suggest that they come in two forms: a kind of moral and intellectual cowardice over security concerns and a conceptual formulation of students as exceptionally vulnerable. Jane Weston Vauclair explores two incidents of equivocation by universities over discussing the radical French magazine *Charlie Hebdo* in a climate cautiously concerned about causing offence. She suggests that a Weberian ethics of responsibility has eroded freedom of enquiry and debate and helped make *Charlie Hebdo* a taboo subject among academics. Other appropriate subjects of discussion have become problematic in the seminar room due to concerns about the vulnerabilities of students. Kathryn Ecclestone and Jenny Jarvie each explore what this sensitivity to emotional and psychological harm means for the education of the next generation and for academic freedom. Jason Walsh's essay joins together the threat posed by security concerns and claims to vulnerability in his passionate assault on the prevailing ontological approach of postmodern academics. He indicates that developing an understanding that social context cannot be divorced from – and should not subsume – either individual agency or actual events will help to build a more robust case for academic freedom.

Academic freedom matters for all the reasons that the AAUP outlined in 1915. But it matters more now as we reflect upon the lessons of the last century. The twentieth century saw shameful McCarthyite crackdowns and periods of student free speech radicalism on campus. Contexts shift but the principle remains. Today, many profess support for academic freedom while marking and policing its limits. Whether you think that freedom of thought and expression are mortally threatened on campus, or not, academic freedom is still a principle that needs be defended.

In the face of good-intentioned and morally-driven censors, the requirement is more rather than less urgent.

References

American Association of University Professors. (2016) *History of the AAUP.* Available at: http://www.aaup.org/about/history-aaup (accessed 12/01/16).

Dewey, J. (1984 [1936]) 'The Social Significance of Academic Freedom' in *Education Digest* pp. 37–39.

Diner, S. J. (1998) *A Very Different Age: Americans of the Progressive Era.* New York: Hill and Wang.

Dworkin, R. (1996) 'We Need a New Interpretation of Academic Freedom' in *Academe* 82 (May-June 1996).

Haskell, T. (1996) 'Justifying the Rights of Academic Freedom' in L. Menand (ed.) *The Future of Academic Freedom.* Chicago: University of Chicago Press pp. 43–90.

Jacoby, R. (2013) 'Stanley Fish Turned Careerism into a Philosophy' in *New Republic* (22/08/13) https://newrepublic.com/article/114224/stanley-fish-careerism (accessed 12/01/16).

Menand, L. (1996) 'The Limits of Academic Freedom' in L. Menand (ed.) *The Future of Academic Freedom.* Chicago: University of Chicago Press pp. 3–20.

Novick, P. (1988) *That Noble Dream: The 'Objectivity Question' and the American Historical Profession.* Cambridge: Cambridge University Press.

Ryan, A. (1995) *John Dewey and the High Tide of American Liberalism.* New York: WW Norton & Co.

Salaita, S. (2015) *Uncivil Rites: Palestine and the Limits of Academic Freedom.* Chicago: Haymarket Books.

Tiede, H-J. (2015) '"To Make Collective Action Possible": The Founding of the AAUP' in *Journal of Academic Freedom.* Vol. 5.

Whitfield, S. J. (1974) *Scott Nearing: Apostle of American Radicalism.* New York: Columbia University Press.

Wiebe, R. (1967) *The Search for Order 1877-1920.* New York: Hill and Wang.

Part One

What is Academic Freedom?

Between Golden Ageism and Prometheanism

Philip Cunliffe

This essay is not so much concerned directly with defending academic freedom so much as establishing the strongest possible basis on which to fight for academic freedom in the future. I try to do this by identifying two typical problems with the way in which academic freedom is often defended by its partisans today. These two defensive manoeuvres I have stylised as 'golden ageism' and 'Prometheanism'. In what follows, I identify the typical traits of these two defensive responses and discuss what is wrong with them. My hope is that the process of clarifying these problems will help identify what a stronger and more consistent vision of academic freedom could look like.

This essay is therefore an exercise in house clearing, justified on the basis that those concerned with academic freedom must get their own house in order before we seek not just to defend but also to fight for and expand the remit of academic freedom. I finish the essay by arguing that the partisans of academic freedom must be bolder not just in defending academic freedom but in fighting for it. There is still much to fight for.

Golden ageism

Academic freedom is often most visible when it is being transgressed or infringed, with the result that conceptually, it is mostly articulated as something inherently defensive. Thus academic freedom is cast as a reaction against external encroachments on the rights of academics to research and teach as they see fit, whether these encroachments come from the market, the state, internal management structures within the university, or censorious student bodies and disciplinary associations within the wider academy. Sometimes, in a rallying mode, the defence of academic freedom is seen as mounting rescue operations, as with attempts to defend a beleaguered individual or minority group within the academy. An example of this practice occurred in 2014 when academics rallied to the defence of the American scholar Steven Salaita who had a job offer rescinded following comments he had made on social media about role of the Israel in the 2014 war in Gaza.

What typifies all these different kinds of practices of academic freedom is that they are reactive and defensive. Often these defensive manoeuvres invoke a time in which academic freedom was more secure. I call this the 'golden ageist' defence and it is problematic in harking back to an era when academic freedom was supposedly unchallenged. To be sure, it is recognised as a problem by defenders of academic freedom. In an interview for *New Humanist*, Stefan Collini insisted that his defence of academic freedom was not nostalgic: 'One of the things I would want to say very emphatically is that I am not taking a nostalgic position' (Taylor, 23/02/12). He goes on to claim that if his book,

What are Universities For?, 'were not signed by someone who teaches at the University of Cambridge it would have a different response [...] Sussex would be better. Greenwich or Teesside better still'. So, how can we avoid golden ageism?

On one level, golden ageism is an understandable response. When defending a line that is being encroached by hostile opponents, it is reasonable that defenders will refer to that time before the threat was manifest, the time before the line was crossed. However, as with all golden ageist responses in whatever practice or field, the first problem is that the golden age never existed. There never was a bucolic time when neighbours knew each other, people did not lock their doors at night, and academics were free from threats to their professional integrity, collective unity and right to free speech. It is the conceit of every generation to imagine that their problems are uniquely terrible and threatening compared to those of the past. While such conceits may be understandable and rousing, they are not excusable. Nor, more importantly are they a viable basis on which to fight for, rather than merely defend, academic freedom.

More broadly, the problem with academic golden ageism is that it is essentially conservative, which is to say reactive. As a conservative response, this defence of academic freedom will always be defined by what it is opposed to, flinching in anticipation of the blows it expects to receive, the prohibitions it expects to encounter. As a result, academics sacrifice the possibility of shaping the future in favour of preserving what they already have. All initiative and energy is directed towards the opponents of academic freedom – whether that be fear-mongering politicians fostering paranoia about extremists on campus, government securocrats seeking to expand the machinery and remit of the surveillance state, academic bureaucrats seeking to tighten their grip on their departmental fiefdoms or managers imported from the corporate world trying to reshape universities into businesses.

As with all conservative responses, this defensive disposition breeds nostalgia. In England, this nostalgia typically takes the form of a longing for the Oxbridge senior common room and college cloisters – the longing often felt even by those who never experienced it. An essay by Terry Eagleton for the *Chronicle of Higher Education* evokes this nostalgia:

> When I first came to Oxford 30 years earlier [...] professionalism would have been greeted with patrician disdain. Those of my colleagues who had actually bothered to finish their Ph.D.'s would sometimes use the title of 'Mr.' rather than 'Dr.,' since 'Dr.' suggested a degree of ungentlemanly labor. Publishing books was regarded as a rather vulgar project [...] College tutors might not even have bothered to arrange set tutorial times for their undergraduates. Instead, the undergraduate would simply drop round to their rooms when the spirit moved him for a glass of sherry and a civilized chat. (Eagleton, 23/04/15)

As Eagleton goes on to admit, the intellectual freedoms of the old academic elite always rested more on their privileges than the strength of their commitment to disciplinary debate or intellectual pluralism:

> Precisely because Oxbridge colleges are for the most part premodern institutions, they have a smallness of scale about them that can serve as a model of

decentralized democracy, and this despite the odious privileges they continue to enjoy. (Eagleton, 23/04/15).

The nostalgic defence of academic freedom eventually burns itself out leaving only the ashes of quietism, as the perpetual task of defence exhausts its protagonists. As Eagleton concedes at the end of his essay, 'Until a better system emerges, however, I myself have decided to throw in my lot with the hard-faced philistines and crass purveyors of utility' (Eagleton, 23/04/15).

Last but not least, golden ageism also misconceives the nature of the challenge to academic freedom – for it does not unfortunately only come from 'outside' the academic sphere – from corporations, government-sponsored marketisation or bureaucratic expansion. It also comes from within – from the erosion of claims to objectivity and truth by epistemological relativism and the politicisation of disciplinary knowledge – views that undercut any viable justification for an independent sphere of inquiry that necessitates an institutional separation from state and market. These internal challenges to academic freedom are beyond the scope of this essay; the only issue here being that golden ageism underestimates the scale of the challenges to academic freedom.

If academics can rid themselves once and for all of the gnawing suspicion that things were better in the past, the fight for the future of the academy can be conducted with greater clarity and vigour.

Prometheanism

The second trap in seeking to defend academic freedom is what I have called the Promethean defence. Named for the classical humanist icon, this second vision of academic freedom invokes the mythical Greek hero condemned to eternal torment by the gods for bringing humanity enlightenment and technology – the secular patron saint of science. When the stakes are so high and the threats to academic freedom so multifarious and insidious, again it is understandable that the defenders of academic freedom would seek to rally the cause by dramatising the stakes.

The Promethean defence of academic freedom typically identifies iconic figures as analogues for Prometheus – heroic personalities persecuted for the challenges they posed to obscurantism, condemned to be appreciated only after their lifetimes, whose insight and achievements reverberate across generations even if they are oppressed and despised while they live. Galileo Galilei is the most typical figure here, the astronomer persecuted by the Church and whose revolutionary discoveries helped establish the modern world.

The Promethean defence is future-oriented because it makes a case for intellectual pluralism in the here and now in order to facilitate the emergence of Prometheans for the future. Such an argument was made by Adam Kissel at a conference on academic freedom held at the University of Kent in March 2015. Here, Kissel argued that academic freedom had to be seen as part of a 'thousand-year plan' – institutional protections are necessary to defend the emergence of knowledge whose gains may only be evident from the vantage point of the future. The freedom of academics to teach and research as they please is necessary because we cannot know in advance what specific piece of research might turn out to be the most important and significant aspect of the expansion of knowledge. Kissel cited the figure of Galileo as evidence of the need for the 'thousand year' defence.

Kissel's reference to Galileo is in keeping with this line of defence: Galileo is the classic Promethean icon and representative of academic freedom. Indeed, the controversies associated with Galileo's scientific discoveries are often taken as inaugurating academic freedom as a distinctive concept, as first articulated by Tommaso Campanella in his 1622 *The Defence of Galileo* (in Hofstader, 2003, p. 59). Taking the model of Galileo then, with reference to academic freedom we might say that the individual who most pointedly challenges the conventional wisdom of the day may turn out to be the hero of the future, set to revolutionise our understanding of the natural and social worlds. In order to maximise the opportunities for the advancement of knowledge, we benefit the most in the long run if we allow diversity of views, methods and approaches to flourish in the academy, along with the confrontations that inevitably follow. Here, the defenders of academic freedom rally to the defence of such individuals, however unpopular their views may be, or alternatively academics seek to defend the conditions in which such individuals can emerge.

The Promethean defence of academic freedom certainly has more to commend it than the golden ageist defence; it entails a positive vision of intellectual vibrancy, flourishing, the subversion and overthrow of orthodoxy, all of which are appealing in and their own right and worth defending of themselves. Yet while defending intellectual diversity and maverick individuals must be both a necessary and large part of the defence of the academy, it is not sufficient. Taken on its own, such a defence also risks collapsing into the conservative traits associated with golden ageism as discussed above.

There are several problems with the Promethean defence. For a start, the Promethean defence is based on an appeal to heroic, isolated individuals, thereby playing to the conceit of scholars as to the significance and potentially enduring appeal of their work. It must be remembered that revolutions cannot be pre-emptively accommodated or contained. By their nature they tend to emerge outside established institutions, whether that be the Church of Galileo's day or the glass-fronted universities of today. The notion that Galileo's intellectual challenge could find an institution broad enough to accommodate both him and the Church is the most utopian of intellectual illusions. Intellectual revolutions on the scale of Galileo's reverberate across and transform society, shattering institutions in their wake.

However sympathetic we may be to the Galileos, revolutionaries must of necessity fight their own battles and their welcome victories will mean sweeping away not only obscurantist intellectual traditions and theories, but also the institutions that shelter them. Perversely, if we were to take the Promethean defence of academic freedom to its logical conclusion it would mean no real revolutions at all. For an academy that was capable of containing scientific and intellectual revolutions on the Galilean scale within its walls would not be an academy at all, but rather a totalitarian institution that was able to absorb, contain and circumscribe all dissent. The corollary of such an institution would be a society that was insulated from the necessarily disruptive reverberations of such dramatic changes in human thought.

Intellectual diversity is good in and of itself, and there are plenty of necessary lesser intellectual revolutions, as well as confrontations and challenges and subversions that must take place in the academy and that necessarily fall short of Galilean standards. It is for these former, more contained and limited clashes that intellectual diversity within the academy is needed. Thus academic freedom is needed for the development of knowledge within the academy, as well as being an essential buttress of freedom of speech in society more widely. The academy is not, should not and cannot be a revolutionary institution. Flowing from this, the defence of academic freedom needs to be rooted in the practices of scholarship rather than a Promethean mythos. In short, defending academic freedom by reference only to the academy's most important intellectual achievements concedes too much to those who want the academy to justify itself by its 'relevance' and its direct and obvious 'impact' on social development.

Whatever they may think about their own work, most academics will never be as fortunate as to be cast in the role of tragic hero in the Promethean drama. Prometheanism in short, has no bearing on the reality of most academic work. For most academics, their work (at least at its best), is and should be narrow, expert, technical, judicious, modest and incremental, building solidly on the achievements of the past and extending the frontiers of knowledge and understanding. Its significance will be most evident to those who have mastered the requisite body of knowledge, in other words, to other academics. This is the ordinary progress of most scholarly knowledge. It is for these academics that academic freedom is worth preserving and more importantly, fighting for. Their work is also the work that will be swept away by the Galileos of the future – and it is this far more modest level of scholarship that is threatened by contemporary challenges to academic freedom.

Fighting for academic freedom

If these are the problems with two typical defences of academic freedom, what are the benefits of going beyond them? The most obvious boon is the possibility of fighting for rather than merely defending academic freedom. In place of the response in which academics are always on the back-foot reacting against external assaults and challenges, academics should think about what a positive vision of academic freedom would look like. What would a positive vision of academic freedom look like within our own institutions, and what kind of a society and polity should these institutions inhabit? Defending academic freedom is an inevitable part of fighting for it; but fighting for academic freedom should mean more than defending it.

The good news is that a golden age might lie ahead of us rather than being irretrievably lost in a musty senior common room in some obscure Oxbridge college. To abandon golden ageism should be to embrace a positive vision of academic freedom with arguments to be made and institutions to be built, rather than defending isolated bastions and beleaguered individuals. To abandon Prometheanism should be to root academic freedom in the actual practice of routine but ultimately and collectively no less important scholarship. For academic freedom to enter the twenty-first century, it means abandoning nostalgia for the past and the conceits of Prometheanism.

References

Eagleton, T. (2015) 'The Slow Death of the University' in *The Chronicle of Higher Education* (23/04/15). Available at: http://chronicle.com/article/The-Slow-Death-of-the/228991/ (accessed 27/11/15).

Hofstader, R. (2003) *Academic Freedom in the Age of College,* London: Transaction Publishers.

Taylor, L. (2012) 'Laurie Taylor's interviews: What's wrong with the university? Laurie Taylor interviews Stefan Collini' in *New Humanist* (23/02/12). Available at: https://newhumanist.org.uk/articles/2760/whats-wrong-with-university-laurie-taylor-interviews-stefan-collini (accessed 30/11/15).

Academic Freedom and the 'Truth Function'

Alan Ryan

This essay breaks no new ground, but draws on familiar components of a liberal theory of freedom of thought and speech to illuminate some peculiarities of academic freedom as distinct from social and political freedom in general. Its underlying purpose, however, is to offer a 'liberationist' defence of liberal education in terms that are central to contemporary discussions, but were less salient for its earliest defenders. The topic wears a different face in different countries; what follows is most obviously relevant to Britain, the British Commonwealth, and the United States, but I hope not irrelevant elsewhere. Indeed, it relies on the German concepts of *Lernfreiheit* and *Lehrfreiheit* to explicate the distinctiveness of academic freedom. I take it for granted that a society where State or Church can insist that everyone toes the line of the local political or religious orthodoxy on pain of dismissal, prison, or death violates academic freedom in the course of violating innumerable other freedoms; our topic here presupposes a liberal democracy rather than a totalitarian dictatorship as background.

What follows relies on John Dewey's notion that universities serve what in 1902 he called 'the truth function', and explores all too briefly what kind of truth, or truths, is at stake. In 1915, Dewey was one of the founders of the American Association of University Professors (AAUP) of which he was the first president, and helped to draw up the statement on academic freedom that was modified in 1940 and again in 1970, but which after a century continues to inspire the AAUP view of what academic freedom consists in. In spite of this role, and fifty-six years working in universities, Dewey wrote little about university education beyond tetchy responses to the provocations of R.M. Hutchins and Mortimer Adler, the provocations including Adler's implausible claim that progressive education was more of a threat to the United States than Adolf Hitler.

A peculiarity of academic freedom in the United States is that it was defined against the background of the widely accepted freedom of an employer to hire and fire at will. By default, American employees are 'at will' employees; but where contractual or statutory provisions require it employers must go through more elaborate procedures before they can terminate an employee. The creation of the tenure system in the United States transformed the status of professors from 'at will' to 'for cause' employees: they could be dismissed only for good reason. Good reason is defined both contractually and in terms of the understood implications of the duties of an academic. In the hundred years since the AAUP published its statement on academic freedom and set up 'Committee A' on academic freedom and tenure to investigate threats to both by university presidents and boards of trustees, there has been wholesale legislative and judicial reconstruction of employer-employee relations in other areas of employment. In the United States, the National

Labour Relations Board established under the New Deal can force employers to recognise trade unions and penalise unfair hiring and firing practices; in Britain, employment tribunals hear complaints of unfair dismissal and oppressive working conditions in any area of employment. Employees of academic institutions who are not protected by legislation specific to academic faculty can use such remedies as they would in any other employment situation, as can academic employees complaining of managerial misconduct. Much else is covered by anti-discrimination legislation and the Human Rights Act 1998; in an American context, Title VI of the Civil Rights Act of 1964 and Title IX of the Education Amendment Act of 1972 are crucial, although their focus is on equal treatment and non-discrimination rather than academic freedom.

The rationale for such legislation and the institutional arrangements associated with it is twofold. First is the establishment of a degree of security in employment. Barely a century ago, workers in the London docks were hired on a half-daily basis. They showed up in the morning and as many as were wanted were hired; the process was repeated in the afternoon, so a docker stood to be unemployed twice a day. There are other notoriously insecure professions whose members excite no sympathy; actors and barristers live not so much hand to mouth as play to play and case to case, but as Adam Smith pointed out, the great rewards going to the successful ensure that there are always plenty of volunteers ready to take their chances. Dockers, paid miserably for appallingly hard labour when in work, and liable to hunger and homelessness when out of work, were very different. If security was one goal, the other was something like enforcing a degree of fair play in the way employers treat their employees. It is for the most part not a matter of curtailing legitimate managerial prerogatives; their existence is taken for granted even when their boundaries are disputed. It is a matter of ensuring that they are exercised in a fashion that respects the dignity as well as the safety of the employee.

Many considerations written into law and forming grounds for taking an employer to a tribunal are not directly freedom-oriented, but may promote social freedom more broadly construed. The prohibition of ethnic, racial, and religious discrimination in hiring and firing represents a social and political decision to sacrifice some of the freedom of employers to hire and fire whomever they choose in favour of an ideal of free and fair opportunity, sacrificing the freedom of the more powerful to enhance the freedom of the less. All such arrangements have their costs, are open to exploitation in obvious ways, and operate only imperfectly. The point of mentioning them in this context is not to discuss their merits and how they might be improved, but to distinguish aspects of employment and employment protection common to all employees, academic and not, from those that are specific to academic employees, that is, to teaching and research faculty. The academic freedom of students will occupy us in due course. It is worth reiterating, however, that none of this legislation focuses directly on issues of free speech, although of course the British Human Rights Act covers that along with many other topics from the prohibition of torture to respect for family life. There is a temptation to conflate the two because anyone complaining that they have been dismissed for their political opinions is, in effect, asserting both that the only grounds for dismissal must be misconduct or incompetence in the academic sphere, *and* that the threat of dismissal is a violation of their rights of free speech.

The thought that academic faculty are entitled to special protection for reasons peculiar to the work they do was not 'natural' to American higher education, and for very different reasons, academic freedom was until recently a non-issue in British higher education. In the introduction to this volume, Cheryl Hudson explains the gaps in the familiar tale linking the establishment of the AAUP to Stanford University's dismissal of E. A. Ross in 1900. Peremptory sackings were not unusual in higher education, although most cases of dismissal for something other than sexual or financial misconduct occurred when a faculty member fell foul of the trustees' – or sometimes the local press's – dislike of his religious views. The right of presidents and trustees to terminate faculty at will was not challenged. They were employees, and that was that. What was unusual about Ross was that he did not take his dismissal lying down, and that he had powerful allies. Half a dozen distinguished professors resigned from Stanford, including A.O. Lovejoy, another founder of the AAUP. Ross appealed to the newly formed American Economic Association, and they duly censured Mrs Stanford's conduct. A further connection between these events and the AAUP's *Declaration* of 1915 is that E.A. Seligman chaired both the committee that investigated Ross's sacking and the committee that drafted the 1915 *Declaration*. If the affair did not immediately inspire the creation of the AAUP, it certainly lodged in the consciousness of its creators, including A.O. Lovejoy and Dewey.

Because the AAUP was founded during a period of American history in which free speech generally was under threat, with the activities of radicals of all stripes being put under pressure both more and less violent, it is easy to conflate the defence of academic freedom with the defence of the First Amendment in the United States, and with liberal political values in Britain. In fact, it was not. Although commentators and judges have assimilated the two, they can be separated both in theory and in practice. After all, the origins of the idea of academic freedom lie in nineteenth-century Germany; *Lehrfreiheit*, or 'freedom of teaching and research' was the liberty of professors to research in whatever areas they were competent in, and to teach as they chose in those areas. The state that enshrined these values was not quite a military autocracy, but it was not very far off. *Lernfreiheit* was the liberty of students to study where they chose and what they chose. It was up to their universities to decide if they had learned enough to secure a diploma, but it was up to them to decide what they wanted to study. The question never arose in Britain, for reasons that remain obscure, and are clearly different in the case of the ancient universities of Oxford and Cambridge, and the 'civic' universities established in cities such as London and Manchester, and different again in the much older universities of Scotland. But, direct political interference was rare, impossible in Oxford and Cambridge, and largely blocked by university charters elsewhere; and, of course, unlikely to come from non-existent billionaire donors like John D. Rockefeller.

Academic freedom, then, consists of three elements, individual and collective, and as one writer on the subject has described it, more nearly a 'guild privilege' than a human right. Individuals (with tenure) have something very like *Lernfreiheit*: within the limits of their contractual duties, they may choose how they teach what they have agreed to teach, and decide how to pursue the research they have said they will pursue. Universities may choose whom to employ, assess their competence, promote and in extremis dismiss them on their own best judgement. It is more akin to the protections that surround the practice of law and medicine, and shield practitioners from lay interference and their professional judgement from inexpert second-guessing. It relies on two challengeable premises and one fragile factual belief.

The first and crucial premise is that a clear line can be drawn between someone's activities as a competent professional and their activities as an engaged citizen, such that a court will defer to their professional judgment in teaching and research, and a university will not penalise their extra-curricular activities by dismissing them; the second is that the profession is better placed to police its members in their professional activities than are university administrators and trustees. Here the analogy with law and medicine runs into difficulty; the British Medical Association can take away an incompetent practitioner's meal-ticket, but no such power lies in the hands of the AAUP or the University College Union, nor is there an equivalent of 'disbarring'. The fragile factual belief is that the public interest in research and tertiary teaching is best served by 'hands-off' regulation. The fragility of this claim is that the defence of academic freedom is a functional one: that the 'truth function' is best served by allowing the faculty who perform that function to decide how to do it. As things have developed, professors with tenure in the United States are more immune from 'outside' regulation than their former peers in law and medicine;

the security of tenured professors in their posts is almost absolute and a source of anxiety to university administrators who wish that their elderly employees would retire and make room for fresh blood – and cheaper junior faculty. The insecurity of short-term contract researchers and adjunct faculty, on the other hand, is almost equally absolute. If not hand to mouth, they live course to course.

An element that blurred the line between academic freedom and free speech protection was the insistence, in the AAUP's 1915 *Declaration*, that a professor could not be dismissed for political activities outside the classroom. The implicit bargain has always been that a clear line could and would be drawn between the professional activities of the professor qua academic and the political activities of the professor qua citizen. Turning a lecture into a political demonstration was not to be protected, but sacking a professor for making political speeches in his own time and off the premises was *ultra vires*. A further way in which academic freedom is unlike freedom of speech can be seen by returning to Dewey's functionalist picture of a university. It serves a social function, and that is the truth function. Initially, this was very much the view from the research university, and Dewey's discussion is largely devoted to freedom in research. It is worth pausing for a moment to work through the subject.

Although the Anglophone world expects most research to take place under the umbrella of a university, this is not true elsewhere, where universities are very often seen as tertiary teaching institutions, even if their faculty do research as well; much research takes place in specialised research institutes, frequently paid for and run by government. Even in the Anglophone world, there are numerous research institutes run by government, and there are levels of university provision where teaching is overwhelmingly the purpose of the institution. There are also the private research laboratories of commercial companies, staffed by academically trained scientists but managed and organised with a view to their impact on their parent companies' profits, and also the privately funded 'think tanks' whose research may be driven by pure curiosity but is more often intended to promote a political agenda. The employees of these last institutions, although they may be named as 'fellows' neither have nor expect the protections accorded to academic faculty.

Today, there is also a vast amount of hybrid research contracted out by commercial enterprises to university departments, or to individual members of university departments, many of whom are impressively entrepreneurial. Under these conditions, the truth function may well be subsumed under the profitable patent generation function. There are well-known and much-discussed problems about the risk of eroding the intellectual probity of researchers whose funders will be happier with positive results than negative ones and eroding the parent university's probity by tempting them to side with commercial funders against unhappy faculty who feel their commitment to revealing what they see as the truth, the whole truth, and nothing but the truth is undermined by funders' insistence on publishing only encouraging results.

The way in which academic freedom is compromised in this new world is roundabout, and varies a great deal between one university and another, and still more between countries. It is not on a par with Stalin having Lysenko's major critic, Nikolai Vavilov detained and starved to death, and all criticism of Lysenkoism criminalised. Nonetheless, there is a route between the pressure to please commercial funders and the violation of what the AAUP and Dewey earlier took to be an implication of academic freedom: that research should be guided only by the competent researcher's best understanding of the most fruitful avenues of investigation. The basis of the researcher's authority was deference to attested expertise. Many late nineteenth-century private American universities, such as Stanford and Chicago, were the creation of rich men of strong opinions, and the model they found congenial was not the self-governing medieval community of scholars surviving in Oxford and Cambridge, but the top-down managerial model of the businesses in which they had made their money. They were happy to promote the modern version of godliness and good learning, but less willing to underwrite research that implied that their wealth was ill-gotten.

Today, direct political interference by the well-off is less visible, but other sorts of near-corruption exist: confidentiality clauses that reduce or remove a researcher's ability to publish whatever they have found out, may literally be bad for the public's health when damaging results about drugs come to light only belatedly. The generosity of rich men with strong political opinions may come with strings attached, even if it is only in the form of demanding a seat on appointment committees and the like. Worse, from the point of view of the individual academic in STEM subjects, the requirement to bring in substantial research grants may form part of a faculty member's contract, and they will face dismissal if they fail to do it. The ability of university administrators to hide behind these considerations if they wish to get rid of faculty they dislike for whatever reason is an evident problem. To my eye, political interference is with one major exception less of a problem in Britain than financial pressures on the one hand and an intellectual climate over-concerned with the emotional comfort of students and faculty who are, or profess to be, distressed by the discussion of dangerous topics.

The three components of academic freedom as conventionally understood embrace the freedom to conduct research under the banner of the quest for the truth about the world, the freedom to organise one's teaching as one chooses, subject to a professional consensus about what counts as an adequate syllabus, carefully taught and intelligently examined, and the right of the faculty not to be second-guessed about hiring, promotion and dismissal. Tenure is the other face of these freedoms; it protects the right of faculty members to a say in the operations of their university. Interestingly, the AAUP wrote into its *Declaration* of 1915 the right of faculty members to criticise their institution's management; this is strikingly at odds with the practice of commercial enterprises. There is no comparable assertion of a right to criticise one's managers in the documents that constitute British assertions of academic freedom, and this may be a serious weakness.

There is another conception of academic freedom appropriate to liberal education, however, which illuminates other pressures on freedom in the academy, and suggests that the belief that one can readily distinguish the freedom of the professor – a guild privilege – from the freedom of the citizen – enshrined in bills of rights and civil rights legislation – may be over-optimistic. To begin with the 'liberationist' ideal of liberal education, then, we might say that the standard defence of academic freedom is largely defensive. That is, the academic community believes that it can get on with its life in a socially responsible way, performing the truth function as it sees it, if it is protected from non-academically warranted interference. The liberationist defence of liberal education, on the other hand, is essentially positive and expansionist; it starts from the thought that although a great deal of intellectual life must begin with rote learning of a pretty mechanical kind – analogous to learning scales if you intend to be a serious pianist – the object is to foster the free exercise of an individual intelligence, to liberate creativity, and to allow the student or new researcher to take full intellectual ownership of their ideas. This is Kant's *'sapere aude'* in action, and the enlightenment theory of education in a snapshot. It requires self-discipline and the recognition of impersonal standards of success; highly creative mathematicians cannot just make things up, nor for that matter can teachers of creative writing. But, the guiding thought is that some or many of us, perhaps most of us, but certainly not all of us very much need to find out not only which of the cultural resources made available by a really good education we can make use of, but how far we can go in emulating and perhaps surpassing their creators.

In what sense is this part of the 'truth function'? Here we are more nearly in the territory of Mill's essay *On Liberty* than Dewey's. The argument for maximal freedom of thought and expression and restrictions only to prevent harm to others was certainly meant by Mill to rest on utilitarian considerations: only such freedom would foster the discovery of new truths about the world. But this was what one might call a tame defence of intellectual freedom. The less tame view was that unless we are exposed to contradiction our beliefs are not really *ours*. If we are content to recite what someone in authority has told us, we need only the skills of a parrot, or what Mill called 'the ape-like faculty of imitation'. If this view has a utilitarian justification, it is very indirect. It insists that from the perspective of an entire society, censorship is always a bad bargain. It does not deny that people whose most cherished views are contradicted very much dislike the experience. But, it resists the thought that their dislike should license any silencing of the opinions complained of on two grounds. One is that coercion is justified only to prevent harm, and dislike is not properly a harm. It is this to which we shall have to return. The other is more genuinely a direct consequentialist argument; only unfettered discussion produces intellectual progress.

Of course, all such arguments are to be read contextually. Your right to challenge my Trinitarian beliefs is not a right to accost me at the bus stop and prevent me leaving until I have heard your unitarian rantings. We are assuming the context of a classroom and that the plausibility of the doctrine of the Trinity is relevant to the course of study, that I have signed up for the course and so on. Ordinary courtesy and perhaps something more dictates that you do not take advantage of my Trinitarian susceptibilities to make me miserable for your own sadistic pleasure; one can defend free speech without defending gratuitous cruelty. But, academic freedom must at least embrace your right to set out the arguments against my Trinitarian beliefs, no matter how deeply I hold them. We can now enter some dangerous contemporary territory. The first concerns the line I draw, following Mill, between dislike and discomfort and genuine harm.

Recently, there has been a lot of discussion, almost all anecdotal, about students demanding 'trigger warnings', and sometimes insisting that some books or topics are taken off a syllabus because they will 'trigger' disabling flashbacks in students who claim to have suffered some form of abuse in the past. It is worth noting that this argument tries to pass Mill's test. It is not simply dislike, but a disabling condition. We do not need to deny that this is sometimes true. We can respect both a student's right not to take a course and a teacher's right to determine its content; just as a particularly squeamish student should not study a subject that involves spending long afternoons dissecting human corpses, so someone vulnerable to triggering events should not attempt to study a subject such as modern American literature that is likely to provoke the reaction. What is out of order is any attempt to dictate what is to be taught and what everyone else is to learn.

Further down the track lies the issue of a teacher's extra-curricular activities and statements. The ongoing case of Steven Salaita, dismissed from the University of Illinois for some intemperate criticisms of Israeli treatment of the Palestinians, is a case in point. Might a Zionist student have a good case for being spared Salaita's presence in the classroom? The AAUP's line suggests a clear 'No' as the answer. US law is ambiguous; 'creating a hostile atmosphere' in the classroom is certainly a ground for dismissal, and both women and minority students have launched law suits against universities and colleges claiming that they have failed to protect them from a hostile atmosphere. I take it, though others certainly do not agree, that this is a pure case of there being an onus on the teacher to ensure civility in the classroom, but no obligation to refrain from his or her extra-curricular activities as long as they are not otherwise unlawful. Incitement is a criminal offence, not a case of academic misconduct; but giving a student lousy grades on ethnic, racial, or religious grounds is anyway grounds for dismissal. A student whose views are deeply at odds with his or her instructor's may find it hard to believe that they will be treated fairly, but that is their tough luck, just as it will be the instructor's tough luck having to be fair. The point of insulating the classroom from the forum is to allow, indeed to force, participants to leave their identities as whatever it might be that is most salient to them outside the door. Neither students nor their teachers should appear in the classroom constrained by their extra-academic identities.

That leaves unfulfilled my promise to say something about what I think the most alarming threat to academic freedom is in contemporary Britain and other Anglophone societies. It is the process by which universities have come to see themselves as businesses. Nobody can deny that universities must balance their books and conduct themselves in a financially prudent fashion, nor that too often they have not done so. Nor can one deny that the so-called STEM subjects are essential to a prosperous future. However, there has been a creeping erosion of the idea of a university as a self-governing institution in which presidents, deans, and the like, are seen as administrative hired help to what is in essence a workers' cooperative, and its replacement with an image of the university as a corporation much like any other, in which the president and other administrators resemble the CEO and top managers, answerable, not to the workers whom they manage, but to 'stakeholders', which is to say public funders in the case of Britain and public universities in the United States; to major donors; and to pharmaceutical and other kinds of company who pay for contract research. Such enterprises have never taken kindly to dissent from their employees, and there are ominous signs that British universities are heading down the track of turning disagreement into a sackable offence. Glue managerial incapacity to tolerate dissent onto student unwillingness to confront uncomfortable ideas and you have a recipe, certainly not for Stalinist brutality, but all too plausibly for the kind of Victorian conformism that provoked J. S. Mill to write *On Liberty*.

References

American Association of University Professors. (2015) *Policy Documents and Reports,* John Hopkins University Press. Available at: http://www.aaup.org/report/1940-statement-principles-academic-freedom-and-tenure (accessed 24/01/16).

Dewey, J. (1915) 'Introductory Address to the American Association of University Professors, 1915' in *The Middle Works of John Dewey, 6,* pp. 88–108.

Dewey, J. (1902) 'Academic Freedom' in *Education Review, 23,* pp. 1–14.

Kant, I. (2009) *An Answer to the Question: 'What is Enlightenment?'* London: Penguin Books.

Menand, L. ed. (1996) *The Future of Academic Freedom.* Chicago: Chicago University Press.

Mill, J.S. (2006) *Liberty and the Subjection of Women,* (Alan Ryan ed.) Harmondsworth: Penguin Books.

Towards a Philosophy of Academic Freedom

Dennis Hayes

Freedom of speech has become separated from academic freedom. It is commonplace to say that freedom of speech is a 'civil' freedom that all citizens enjoy but 'academic freedom' is unique to academics. I have heard this from university managers, colleagues and many commentators who want to correct what they see as the conflation of the two in the Academics For Academic Freedom (AFAF) statement of academic freedom:

> (1) That academics, both inside and outside the classroom, have unrestricted liberty to question and test received wisdom and to put forward controversial and unpopular opinions, whether or not these are deemed offensive, and

> 2) That academic institutions have no right to curb the exercise of this freedom by members of their staff, or to use it as grounds for disciplinary action or dismissal (AFAF, 2015)

I drafted this statement in autumn 2006 with the late Roy Harris, Emeritus Professor of General Linguistics at the University of Oxford, with help from Dolan Cummings of the Institute of Ideas and others. At that time, we were specifically challenging the nascent attempts to shut down speech through the challenge that what was being said was 'offensive' to someone because of their religion, beliefs, minority status or simply because they were fragile individuals. The launch of AFAF began with a misleading headline in the *Times Higher Education Supplement* (*THES*): 'Scholars demand right to be offensive' in which it was argued that AFAF supporters wanted 'the "unrestricted liberty" to be offensive to others without fear of sanction' (Baty, 2006). Roy Harris thought that the idea of such a 'right' would be silly. Our opposition was simply to censorship, to the violent, anti-human suppression of speech through the cry 'That's offensive!' and the effect this had on free speech and debate in universities (Hayes, 2006).

Almost a decade on from the launch of AFAF, censorship reached a new height with the shutting up by bloody murder of the *Charlie Hebdo* cartoonists because what they did was 'offensive'. The tragedy of this loss of life is that, after a short time of international revulsion expressed through thousands of Je suis Charlie posts, posters, banners and headlines, the opposition and suppression of anyone or anything deemed to be 'offensive' has grown. Journalists and campaigners like Julie Bindel, *Spiked*'s Brendan O'Neill and Maryam Namazie have been banned from universities or shouted down for views which student groups and universities find offensive (see O'Neill, 2015a and 2015b for these and other examples). Writers and journalists can at least fight back in the press. All those mentioned have done just that, as have many of their supporters.

It seems to be journalists, writers and campaigners, rather than academics who hit the headlines for being controversial. The most recent high-profile academic to make national news was Professor Thomas

Docherty who was suspended from his post at the University of Warwick. But his suspension was not for his controversial writings on the lack of ideas, the bureaucratisation and business-orientation of the modern university (see Docherty, 2011) but for inappropriate body language, sighing and irony (Hayes, 2014). The message of this suspension is 'conform' and do not indicate in any way that you oppose state intervention, institutional procedures or management. You can write about them in books or journal articles but you must not speak up publicly or express disagreement in any way. It is not surprising then that the first ever Free Speech University Rankings (FSUR) produced by *Spiked* in February 2015 showed that 80 per cent of UK universities censor free speech (*Spiked*, 2015).

In such a censorious climate, the Dochertys of this world are few and most academics are entirely compliant and rarely make any public challenge to the instrumentalist and bureaucratic system they work in, which is dominated by increasing numbers of league tables, primarily the Research Excellence Framework (REF) and soon the Teaching Excellence Framework (TEF). Above all, it is the National Student Survey (NSS) which has formally re-oriented academic life around compliance with activities that promote 'student satisfaction' rather than intellectual challenge and critical thinking. It is tempting to talk about cowardly, conformist academics but there is no sense of fear in academia. There is just professionalism and a desire to get on with research and teaching and even to celebrate the global achievements of UK universities. There is no consciousness of conformism and no consciousness of individual or collective cowardice. The academy has simply become dull and the explanation is not merely cultural and psychological. It is the result of the facile separation of freedom of speech from academic freedom. There have been attempts to develop and exploit this supposed distinction in various ways as a challenge to the approach of AFAF. Here are three examples. In the first, statements that tie the concept of academic freedom to freedom of speech – as does the AFAF statement – are simply acknowledged and then ignored:

> Freedom of speech is not the same thing as academic freedom, which involves considerably more than just speech rights (as noted earlier, academic freedom entails the right to teach, research, publish, criticise academic and other institutions in which academics work). (Johnstone, 2012, p. 4)

Because it is just so obvious isn't it? Equally as obvious is the need to override freedom of speech for 'moral' reasons because of the fact that every country restricts speech (Johnstone, 2012, p. 4).

The second example is a variation on this side-lining approach. I refer to Anna Traianou's claim that there are two concepts of academic freedom; the first being when:

> Some commentators effectively treat academic freedom as equivalent to free speech: the freedom of academics and students to speak out on public issues, without attempts to prevent this and without their being penalized for doing so. This relates to public statements as well as to the presentation of personal views in the course of teaching sessions, or in research publications.

The second when:

> By contrast, other writers interpret academic freedom to refer to a form of professional autonomy,

relating to university academics as an occupational group. (Traianou, 2015, pp. 1–2)

This latter concept is the dominant one and what makes academic life so professional and dull.

But even Traianou recognises at the end of her paper there is need at least at the present time to emphasise the free speech concept of academic freedom. It is impossible in any case to uphold a clear distinction between the two concepts. The third and most direct criticism of the AFAF statement, made by David Miller and colleagues, is that it:

> [...] is a narrow absolutist approach. Narrow in the sense of referring only to ideas and their transmission. It has nothing to say about the freedom to research and to teach and nor more significantly of the conditions under which individual and institutional autonomy might be fostered. Including such matters are important to give a breadth to the definition but also to remind us that this is not a question only of the freedom to hold or pass on views but much more fundamentally to do research and to discover that things are not as had been thought.

> Academic Freedom is a matter of thought, ideas, belief, speech and advocacy, but is also a matter of action, behaviour and 'struggle'. This suggests that it is not a matter only of ideas but, perhaps more fundamentally, the right to undertake research, to find things out, to investigate. This is a process involving both ideas, theories and beliefs and actions in the world. (Miller, D., Mills, T. and Harkins, S., 2010, p. 7)

This seems a more 'left wing' approach to the conventional separation of freedom of speech from the professional job of a university employee but despite all the talk of 'struggle' and 'action' in reality this is just a radical gloss on the idea of academic freedom being about the professional role. The authors give away at the outset their guiding belief that in relation to universities and academic freedom: 'the major threats are not questions of freedom of speech' (Miller et al., 2010, p. 1). This is a viewpoint that the AFAF statement directly challenges. The major threats to academic freedom and universities are precisely 'issues of free speech'.

What these criticisms of the AFAF statement lack is any understanding of the historical context in which we talk about academic freedom. We need not go back far in history to see an important shift in our understanding of the relationship between academic freedom and freedom of speech.

In the liberal 1960s and early 1970s there was an easy equation of 'academic freedom' with 'free speech' and 'free expression' and a desire to extend them because of faith in human potential whether it led to socialism or a better form of capitalism. Anthony Arblaster, writing in the Penguin Education Special *Academic Freedom* in 1974, argues that:

> The freedom that matters is the openness of education, that is, the tolerance of a great range and diversity of opinions, not only in relation to specific subjects, but also in relation to education itself, its purposes and methods. [...] In education the freedom to hold opinions, especially unorthodox opinions, and to advocate them openly and without any fear of reprisal, is supremely important.

He adds:

> It is not the business of teachers or educational administrators to set themselves up as arbiters of

the politics or the morality of either staff or students – although they frequently attempt to do so. (Arblaster, 1974, pp. 13–14)

For Arblaster, 'academic freedom' was 'rather a pompous term for freedom of, and within, education' (1974, p. 9) and he had little interest in attempting to differentiate it from freedom of expression.

This equation of 'academic freedom' with free speech and a wide range of freedoms was unproblematic to many, not just to radicals. These were confident times. But to some, and particularly to lawyers and First Amendment scholars in the US, it seemed that academic freedom had lost its meaning. The use of the term was so promiscuous and so wide in its application that, according to the *Encyclopaedia of Higher Education*, it '(in its modern conception, though not in the past) includes the right of the academic individual to engage in political activity' (in Van Alstyne 1972a, pp. 141–2; see also Van Alstyne 1972b).

This was too much for the law professors and in 1972 William Van Alstyne declared, in a paper given at a symposium on academic freedom, that the usage had to regain its ties with the profession or vocation of the academic: 'It is the seemingly small and reactionary purpose of this essay to suggest that this development in the usage of academic freedom was never sound and that it ought now to be abandoned' (Van Alstyne, 1972a, p. 142).

Van Alstyne began a process that led to what I call the 'Van Alstyne settlement', which sees academic freedom as a professional freedom (Hayes, 2015). The Van Alstyne settlement has its UK champion, Eric Barendt, but above all others it is Stanley Fish in the US who promotes the view that academic freedom is just about the job. Fish wants academics to regain a 'narrow sense of vocation' (Fish, 2008a, p. 8). According to Ted Walker, Fish believes he is a lone fighter: 'Academic freedom is a spectrum at one end of which is the 'It's Just a Job' school [...] which treats academics as employees hired to perform a specific job, with freedom limited to that scope' (in Walker, 2012; see also Fish, 2008a; 2008b and Fish, 2014). Fish is wrong and most academics today are members of his school.

Towards a philosophy of academic freedom

The first step towards a philosophy of academic freedom is to ask why freedom of speech is the 'foundational' freedom. The AFAF statement was an attempt to restore unfettered freedom of speech and with it faith in human beings. Then, as now, we saw no issues with academics or ordinary people arguing about anything and everything. That is what freedom of speech means. Barendt has clearly lost faith in the power and importance of free speech and he makes a curious remark that 'it is hard to find a single justification for freedom of speech' (Barendt, 2010, p. 72).

AFAF values freedom of speech as the foundational freedom on which all our other freedoms depend and without which they have no meaning. In contrast, free speech is usually seen as just one freedom among many and sometimes must be traded off in the interest of other freedoms or values. This position is often summarised with the statement that freedom of speech is 'not an absolute' (Lee, 1990, p. 25). I have addressed the many objections to this in arguing for academic freedom 'No Ifs, No Buts' elsewhere (Hayes, 2008, 2009, 2011). Here I want to give an a priori or logical argument to show why free speech is an absolute and then supplement this with an empirical argument.

The a priori or logical argument

What academics have forgotten in their obsession with the research and scholarship in their academic job, is that free speech is a prerequisite for all other freedoms, including theirs. Roy Harris has argued convincingly that 'freedom is, in the first instance, freedom of speech. Freedom of speech is the archetypal freedom' (Harris 2009, p. 125) and:

> The general rationale for giving priority to freedom of speech can be stated very succinctly. For any proposed freedom F, being free may turn out to be an illusion if there has been no opportunity to test the freedom claimed against contrary opinions. In short, we cannot *know* that we enjoy freedom F – we cannot even know what exercising that freedom would be – until F itself has been subjected to and survived unrestricted critical scrutiny. And that in turn requires freedom of speech. For if we rely on anything short of that, the freedom we had imagined we were exercising may be illusory. (Harris, 2009, p. 126)

To take Harris' argument a step further we can say that we do not understand our own opinions unless we present them for criticism. This argument does away with Barendt's claim that 'it is hard to find a single justification for freedom of speech' (2010, p. 72).

The empirical argument

The 'empirical' argument derived from the radical philosopher Tony Skillen, is based on 'claims of "very general facts" about how minds work and the role of discourse in that working' (Skillen, 1982, p. 149). In an impressive attempt to provide a defence of freedom of speech 'on socialist terms' he says this about challenging beliefs:

> One's beliefs are close to the centre of 'who one is' and criticism of them can cut deep and meet protective resistance. But it is of the essence of human rationality that beliefs are held as valid, as justified by their correspondence to what is the case. The mind expresses itself and thus exposes itself to change through criticism. Criticism and discussion respect these dimensions of rationality, whereas silencing smashes at them, practically denying the capacity, not only to have reached views through some process of experience and reflection, but to go beyond them through further formative activity. This contempt applies also to your status as 'hearer' of speech, denying your capacity to reason and reflect on what you hear. You are treated as if words could actually causally affect you in an almost physical way rather than through their according with your grasp of things and thus their being 'acceptable' to you. (Skillen 1982, p. 145)

The perception we have of a young person, a student, and of humanity, is exemplified by the attitude that Skillen castigates as 'contempt' but in its new therapeutic expression it is a 'caring contempt' (see Hayes, 2015). It expresses a profoundly diminished sense of human potential but with added compassion.

Vanessa Pupavac has documented, in a detailed historical and global survey, how the Enlightenment view of all humans as capable of autonomous rational understanding through language and communication has been replaced by what she calls 'linguistic governance'. 'Linguistic governance' expresses a view of humanity as constituted by vulnerable citizens who must be protected from linguistic harm: 'The concept of vulnerability involves anticipatory victimhood and the imperative to take preventative action' (Pupavac, 2012, p. 227). The result is restrictive legislation, speech codes, 'no platform policies' and censorship. These restrictions have gathered strength in the last few years in the name of victims and the vulnerable. The Leveson proposals for press regulation in the UK are the starkest example of this new illiberality which has gained support from hundreds of once liberal academics, writers and actors (Hume, 2012 and 2014).

The loss of the Enlightenment vision of humanity's potential and its replacement by a diminished idea of a human being has led to a decline in the support intellectuals and politicians give to free speech. This decline is paralleled by a decline in academic freedom. Academic freedom is best seen as part of a continuum. A society that values freedom of speech will support the university as a place where academics can take freedom of speech to its fullest expression, not just in giving opinions, but through research and scholarship testing and challenging opinions. If a society ceases to value freedom of speech it will cease to value the university and academic freedom.

It is the collapse in support for free speech that has led to the lack of confidence of academics in academic freedom, fostered by their turn to professionalism. This is why we find Barendt arguing that 'However persuasive the case for academic freedom may be, it is unlikely to enjoy widespread popular support' (2010, p. 5). This is also why he can talk about the 'puzzle' that is 'academic freedom' and ask 'How can academic freedom be justified, granted that it appears to confer special freedoms or rights on certain individuals and institutions?' (Barendt, 2010, p. 5).

If we believe in freedom of speech, we can see that there is nothing elitist or special about academics having freedom of speech above citizen rights because there is something special about academics. This can be illustrated by reference to how it was possible to describe academics at a time when freedom of speech was valued in society. The Australian philosopher John Anderson, writing in 1960, saw academics as adding to societal freedom of speech because of their role:

> The work of the academic, qua academic, is criticism; and, whatever his special field may be, his development of independent views will bring him into conflict with prevailing opinions and customary attitudes in the public arena and not merely among his fellow-professionals. (Anderson, [1960] 1980, p. 214)

This is a confident view of the academic as a social critic stepping beyond the area of his special subject-based expertise. We have lost this confidence (see Dworkin, 1996, p. 197). To regain it requires a defence of freedom of speech. If academics make the case for freedom of speech, academic freedom is likely to enjoy widespread popular support.

Bringing free speech back in

Academics need to be aware of the quietism produced by the current therapeutic culture of safety, exemplified today by the promotion of 'safe spaces' for discussion in universities. They need to be reminded of their duty to question and test received wisdom and to be the societal models of autonomous individuals exercising free speech. They can be uniquely critical human beings because criticism is their work. All that academics need to do is to speak up. Not to speak up about their research merely for purposes of evidencing 'impact' but to engage with wider issues and not be afraid to come into conflict with prevailing attitudes and ideas. The first step in regaining academic confidence is for academics to speak up for freedom of speech, even offensive, hateful and crazy speech and, of course, the right to respond to it with more speech. They should take inspiration from the words of Supreme Court Justice Louis Brandeis summing up in the case of Whitney v. California (1927): 'If there be time to expose through discussion the falsehood and fallacies, to avert the evil by the processes of education, the remedy to be applied is more speech, not enforced silence' (in Winston 2012, p. 341).

When Van Alstyne's symposium paper, with its 'small and reactionary purpose', was written in the 1970s, free speech was an unquestioned good because of belief in human beings, in the potential of ordinary people. In the twenty-first century, freedom of speech is restricted everywhere because of distrust and caring contempt for ordinary people. In the current climate of conformism and censorship, restoring free speech, and therefore academic freedom, is the duty of every scholar.

References

Academics For Academic Freedom. (AFAF) (2015) Statement of Academic Freedom: Available at: www.afaf.org.uk (accessed 9/10/15).

Anderson, J. ([1960]1980) 'The Place of the Academic in Modern Society' in D. Z. Phillips ed., *Education and Inquiry*, pp. 214–221. Oxford: Basil Blackwell.

Arblaster, A. (1974) *Academic Freedom*. Harmondsworth: Penguin Education.

Barendt, E. (2010) *Academic Freedom and the Law: A Comparative Study*. Oxford and Portland, Oregon: Hart Publishing.

Baty, P. (2006) 'Scholars demand right to be offensive' in *Times Higher Education Supplement*, (22/12/06). Available at: https://www.timeshighereducation.com/news/scholars-demand-right-to-be-offensive/207230.article (accessed 09/10/15).

Dworkin, R. (1996) 'We Need a New Interpretation of Academic Freedom' in L. Menand, (Ed.) *The Future of Academic Freedom*. pp. 187–198. Chicago & London: The University of Chicago Press.

Fish, S. (2008a) *Save the World on Your Own Time*. Oxford: Oxford University Press.

Fish, S. (2008b) 'Academic freedom is not a divine right' in *The Chronicle of Higher Education*, (05/09/08). Available at: http://chronicle.com/article/Academic-Freedom-Is-Not-a/10461 (accessed 09/10/15).

Fish, S. (2014) *Versions of Academic Freedom: From Professionalism to Revolution*. Chicago: University of Chicago Press.

Harris, R. (2009) 'Freedom of Speech and Philosophy of Education' in *British Journal of Educational Studies*. 57 (2) June 2009, pp. 111–126.

Hayes, D. (2006) 'Verbal brawling is just what the academy needs' in *Times Higher Education*, (22/06/06). Available at: http://www.timeshighereducation.co.uk/story.asp?sectioncode=26&storycode=207259 (accessed 04/11/15).

Hayes, D. (2008) 'Academic freedom means free speech and no "buts"' in *The Free Society*, (04/03/08).

Hayes, D. (2009) 'Academic freedom and the diminished subject' in *British Journal of Educational Studies*. 57 (2) pp. 127–145.

Hayes, D. (2011) *The 'Limits' of Academic Freedom*. Inaugural Lecture, University of Derby, (30/03/12).

Hayes, D. (2014) 'On the freedom to sigh' in *Spiked*, (23/09/14). Available at: http://www.spiked-online.com/freespeechnow/fsn_article/on-the-freedom-to-sigh#.VjnpbTEnzIU (accessed 04/11/15).

Hayes, D. (2015) 'Academic freedom, free speech and human being' in *Europa World of Learning 2015* (65th Edition), London and New York: Routledge. pp. 11–16.

Hume, M. (2012) *There is No Such Thing As a Free Press… and we need one more than ever.* Exeter: Imprint Academic.

Hume, M. (2014) 'Liberal UK signs its own death warrant' in *Spiked* (24/03/14) Available at: http://www.spiked-online.com/freespeechnow/fsn_article/leveson-liberal-uk-signs-its-own-death-warrant#.U1jdzPldWM4 (accessed 04/11/15).

Johnstone, M-J. (2012) 'Academic freedom and the obligation to ensure morally responsible scholarship in nursing' in *Nursing Inquiry,* (19) pp. 107–115.

Lee, S. (1990) *The Cost of Free Speech.* London: Faber and Faber.

Miller, D., Mills, T. and Harkins, S. (2010) *Teaching About Terrorism: The debate about Academic Freedom,* British International Studies Association Conference, Manchester Conference Centre. Available at: http://bisa.ac.uk/index.php/component/bisa/?task=download_paper&format=raw&passed_paper_id=225 (accessed 09/11/15).

O'Neill, B. (2015a) 'Stepford Students, safe in their little PC world' in *The Independent,* (04/10/15). Available at: http://www.independent.ie/opinion/comment/stepford-students-safe-in-their-little-pc-world-31580241.html (accessed 09/11/15).

O'Neill, B. (2015b) 'Why we must fight for free speech for people we loathe' in *Spiked,* (08/10/15). Available at: http://www.spiked-online.com/newsite/article/Why-we-must-fight-for-free-speech-for-people-we-loathe/17517#.VhfBAzZdHIU (accessed 09/11/15).

Pupavac, V. (2012) *Language Rights: From Free Speech to Linguistic Governance.* London and New York: Palgrave Macmillan.

Skillen, T. (1982) 'Freedom of Speech', in Graham, K. (Ed) *Contemporary Political Philosophy: Radical Studies.* Cambridge: Cambridge University Press: pp. 139–159.

Spiked. (2015) Free Speech University Rankings – a Spiked project: http://www.spiked-online.com/free-speech-university-rankings/analysis#.VhpyEDZdHIV (accessed 09/11/15).

Traianou, A. (2015) 'The Erosion of Academic Freedom in UK Higher Education', *Ethics in Science and Environmental Politics,* 15: pp. 1–9.

Van Alstyne, W. W. (1972a) 'The Specific Theory of Academic Freedom and the General Issue of Civil Liberties', in *Annals of the American Academy of Political and Social Science.* pp. 140–156.

Van Alstyne, W. W. (1972b) 'The Specific Theory of Academic Freedom and the General Issue of Civil Liberty', in Pincoffs, E. L. (Ed) *The Concept of Academic Freedom.* Austin and London: University of Texas Press pp. 59–85.

Walker, T. (2012) 'Defining the boundaries of academic freedom with scholar Stanley Fish', 2012 Campbell Lecture, Rice University. *Rice News* (19/04/12). Available at: http://news.rice.edu/2012/04/19/defining-the-boundaries-of-academic-freedom-with-scholar-stanley-fish/ (accessed 04/11/15).

Winston, B. (2012) *A Right to Offend*, London: Bloomsbury Academic.

Ad Hominem and the Wise Wound

James Heartfield

'STFU and sit down.' This is a common retort in social media rows. Literally, it means 'shut the fuck up' but it actually means, 'I have nothing to learn from you, you will learn from me.' In particular, it indicates that the addressee is excluded from true understanding because of his supposedly privileged position. Someone tweets: 'It is never not a good time to remind cis men to sit down and listen.' ('Cis' means 'cisgendered', which is to say having the gender that you were ascribed at birth, as opposed to transgendered). Of course, all of us should listen carefully to one another, but that is not what this tweeter is saying.

Rebecca Solnit's well-observed essay *Men Explain Things To Me*, gave rise to the short hand 'mansplaining', or, in other words, that irritating and boorish habit men have of pedantically explaining things that they often understand less-well than the women they are talking at. Mansplaining is a witty short hand for a bad habit, but like so many categories it can become a barrier to understanding. The short hand that a man might presume to have knowledge he does not have slides into an assumption that he does not. The category can be extended, too. There is 'whitesplaining', and 'cisplaining', where white or cis people presume to explain to black or trans people what their issues are really about.

Beyond the psychological insight that without self-awareness men often assume the position of expert in relation to women, the short hand 'mansplaining' takes us into another sphere, where the social position of the speaker is assumed to tell us something valuable about the quality of what is expressed. In conventional logical argument, this would be an error, the error of *argumentum ad hominem* (usually shortened to just ad hominem). Arguments that dismiss *what* is being said because of *who* is saying it fail, in this view, because they go to the man, not the argument. In this way of thinking the status of the speaker is just not relevant to the merits of the argument.

Outside of the school of logic, though, other ways of assessing arguments have grown up. In the social sciences, and in communications, 'discourse analysis' has tended to the view that ideas are closely bound up with social positions. Working with a concept of ideology it has been argued that systems of thought are expressive of social factions. This is a positional logic. Sometimes it is called the 'standpoint theory', namely that ideas are expressive of a standpoint. Standpoint theory has not yet collapsed the critique of an idea into the critique of the social position of the person voicing it. It ought to be possible both to criticise an idea in its own right and also to consider it as reflective of a social position – but this point hangs by a very thin thread. Hundreds of thousands of undergraduates are hearing, if they are not being told, that you can assess the validity of an idea by asking 'who does it serve?'

An upside down development of the standpoint theory is the theory that suffering is the basis of insight.

This is the theory of the 'wise wound'. Poets Penelope Shuttle and Peter Redgrove coined the phrase to talk about the spirituality of women and the menstrual cycle. The theory of the wise wound is that the very thing that is a badge of oppression is also the basis of insight. Of course the hidden meaning is that you cannot truly learn anything, because only someone with this special experience can understand what it means.

There is something of the 'wise wound' in Karl Marx's proposition that the property-less classes had 'radical chains'. He was arguing with a fellow philosopher who dismissed the idea that the working classes could attain to that status that Hegel had ascribed to the civil service, of a universal class, that could stand above particular interests, and see the good of the whole nation. Marx is saying that while it might seem that the property-less have no great resources from which to judge the state of things, that itself might be an advantage. As he later put it, the working class had nothing to lose but its chains.

The logical reasoning that dismisses the ad hominem attack on the speaker's position is, in this different register of debate, turned on its head. Now it is very much the case that the speaker, the standpoint of the speaker, is intimately related to the merit of the speech. The late philosopher Richard Rorty thought that this was not really a good argument. Suffering he held, is 'non-linguistic', even bestial, which is why 'there is no such things [sic] as the "voice of the oppressed" [...] the job of putting their situation into language must be done for them' (Rorty, 1989, p. 94).

For the logical point of view, reason is a movement away from immediate experience, whereas for the 'voice of the oppressed' the movement away from immediate experience is suspect, and distorting. For the rationalists, reason takes us away from immediate experience, but towards the truth of things. The senses can deceive. Socrates uses the example of the stick half in and half out of the water. Our senses tell us that the stick is bent. We can see that it is bent. But our reason tells us that the stick is not bent, but that the water acts as a prism distorting the image of the stick. Reason takes us closer to the objective truth (the stick is straight), whereas our senses leave us in the subjective illusion that the stick is bent. So, similarly (though Socrates could not have known) all of us see the sun rise and the sun set, while we know that what we are seeing is in truth the rotation of the earth. The sun is still, relative to us, but we are moving. This shows that reason while taking an initial step away from perceived reality still takes us closer to reality, through the power of reason.

For the rationalists, ideas are abstract, universal, commensurable with one another, and between different people. For the standpoint theorists, the claim of reason to detach itself from immediate experience is always suspect and open to critique. The more stridently the universal is proclaimed, the more one suspects that it hides a particular interest, disguising that as a non-controversial, universal position. 'Oh yes, you say "thou shalt not kill" – but your armies are raining terror on the developing world,' says the undergraduate student in the ethics seminar. Or, as Ralph Waldo Emerson put it, 'The louder he talked of his honor, the faster we counted our spoons' (1860, p. 12).

The impulse to regulate

One clear outcome of the standpoint theory is that speech must be regulated. In this account, a hearing is a limited resource that must be rationed out carefully. In an interview for the *Australian Humanities Review*, Stanley Fish argues that 'When you talk you're talking in the service of something.' Further, he says, 'In any normal situation you speak for a reason: to inform, to command, to acquiesce, to ask a question, to further an agenda, to close an agenda down' (Lowe and Jonson, 01/02/98). As he puts it, speech cannot be separated from its consequences, and therefore it must be regulated: 'speech has a purpose and when we feel this purpose threatened by some of speech's forms, we will always curtail it' (Lowe and Jonson, 01/02/98).

On this account speech must be regulated because it is an action. So, similarly, the American feminist lawyer Catharine Mackinnon argued that pornography is an act of violence. As she puts it in her sarcastically-titled book *Only Words*, pornography is an instruction that leads people to commit rape, as surely as the command 'Kill' leads an attack dog to kill.

In *Towards a Feminist Theory of the State*, Mackinnon argues that women's social inequality in the household comes before, or beneath the formal equality of citizens before the law. For that reason, legal equality will only ever reinforce social inequality. From this she argues that the radicals must use the law to make amends for women's unequal social position. Arguing against the First Amendment right to free speech, Mackinnon helped argue for the Canada Supreme Court's 1992 judgement against pornography – under which many pornographers, including some lesbian pornography, and some art, has been suppressed.

Fish agrees that the First Amendment defence of free speech is wrongly over-extended. It is only there to defend what he calls 'political speech', so that government is not protected from criticism. But this is too narrow a definition of political speech, which comes close to saying that the speech that Fish defends is the speech he agrees with. Mocking the American Civil Liberties Union's stand defending the speech rights of Nazis, Fish calls it 'an organisation whose project is to go out and find things it hates and then grow them' (Lowe and Jonson, 01/02/98).

The direction of standpoint theory is towards the regulation of speech. It is not hard to see why. In this particular account the viewpoint of the oppressed is suppressed and ignored. Free speech simply represents the bad conscience of the dominant ideology. Only the rights of the powerful are defended in the defence of free speech, the argument runs. Current criticisms of academic freedom run along the same lines.

Attempting, like Catharine Mackinnon, to regulate and legislate on what speech ought to be supported and what suppressed is not easy. On campuses in the United Kingdom, college authorities have tended to subcontract the regulation of public debate to students' unions. Students' unions, while often lively and argumentative, are generally under-representative and sometimes declamatory, giving rise to the many examples of censorship discussed elsewhere in this collection.

Historian Evan Smith shows that the early campaign to suppress some political speech took as its target the far right, in the 'no platform for fascists' demand. One can see a certain justification for that position in that fascism is a movement that elevates force over reason. Still, the 'no platform for fascists' turned out to be the small pinprick that burst the free speech balloon on campuses. Certainly I can remember the National Union of Students seeking to have support for Zionism characterised as 'racism', so that Israelis and their supporters would be denied speaking rights. In the 1990s, the Islamist organisation Hizb ut-Tahrir was the target of several motions of 'no platform', on the grounds of its retrograde views of women and homosexuals. Sussex University Students Union even banned a pamphlet on the AIDS crisis by the militant gay campaigner Don Milligan and doctor Michael Fitzpatrick, because it was sceptical about the government's health campaign.

As the many overwrought, and sometimes ridiculous, examples of students' union censorship show, it is not really possible to construct a policy that regulates speech in such a way as to defend the oppressed and suppress the oppressor. The reasons are clear enough. Though the proponents of such bans think that they are appealing to a strong consensus about what is and what is not 'acceptable', that is rarely the case. Some Cardiff University activists thought that there was general agreement that Germaine Greer's views on transgender ruled her out of public debate; they were then surprised that the veteran feminist had many supporters who guaranteed that she did speak. By what right, wondered the activists, did their critics speak on whether trans people existed or not?

Another problem that aggravates the debate over free speech is that many of the proposed bans and 'no platforms' are not really an attempt at constructing a policy framework, but are themselves declamatory, expressive acts. 'We are just expressing our free speech,' say the protestors demanding the ban – except that their demand is that others be silenced.

Intersectionality

Jill: I'm upset that you are upset.

Jack: I'm not upset.

Jill: I'm upset that you're not upset that I'm upset that you're upset.

Jack: I'm upset that you're upset that I'm not upset that you're upset that I'm upset, when I'm not.

Jill: You put me in the wrong.

Jack: I'm not putting you in the wrong.

Jill: You put me in the wrong for thinking you put me in the wrong.

Jack: Forgive me.

Jill: No.

Jack: I'll never forgive you for not forgiving me.

The psychoanalyst R. D. Laing discovered a Twitter exchange twenty years before the birth of the internet – and he found it among his mental patients (Laing, 1971, p. 21).

The contemporary 'call-out' culture appeals to an implied set of values that many students and their unions assume to be commonly held and beyond dispute – these values might broadly be understood to be against discrimination and oppression. However, as others, such as Katha Pollitt, have noted the college-based and online feminist community is pointedly given to violently expressed divisions. Radical feminists attack liberal feminists as collaborators; in turn sex-positive feminists attack radical feminists for their whorephobia – who are then denounced as Trans-Exclusionary Radical Feminists, or TERFs. White feminists were roundly taken to task for their failure to understand the position of Women of Colour. Feminists were disappointed that there were few takers for their invitation to admit to a crisis of masculinity. Male 'allies' were derided as 'brocialists' and would-be 'white knights' who wanted to mansplain where the movement should go.

It should be said that there is a point to the implied critique of liberal feminism by the Feminists of Colour, who are really pointing to the elitist underpinnings of a social movement that is hostile to the greater mass. However, the manoeuvre of 'calling out' white feminists' racism, which seems to have some egalitarian component, in fact only drives the logic of disintegration and division of further. We might say that all the critiques have some point to them. The Radical Feminists' women-only space is a retreat. Male allies are indeed ridiculous. But all of them lead towards division and are reflected in divisions between student groups on campus.

Pointedly, most of these debates are about 'recognition' and respect: that is less about the distribution of material resources, more about the psychic wage. Issues that preoccupy the social justice warriors on campus are insults and exclusions; individual acts of violence are highlighted, but more so are threats of violence, and online harassment. Twitter and hyper-alert students' unions are not the cause of the retreat into reactive and mutually opposed positions. They are merely the vehicles that are best suited to the reactive and under-considered exchange. The exchange is interminable, because consent is impossible.

German Sociologist Axel Honneth thought hardest about the struggle for mutual recognition. He was drawing on Hegel's dialectic of the Master and the Slave.

Hegel showed that the struggle for recognition would be won by the combatant who put his honour above his life, and lost by the one who put his life above his honour. This is the origin of the spiritual existence of man – honour – as a value higher than mere animal existence.

Still, said Hegel, the Master's victory, and the subsequent respect he wins are unsatisfying because it is victory over, and the respect of, a slave. Hegel sees the primitive philosophies of the Stoics, the Cynics and the Early Christians as different, and mutually exclusive attempts by slaves to understand their condition. The escape from that condition, however, does not come through thought, but by the transcendent principle, which for Hegel is labour. The labour of the slave begins as a torment, and a humiliation, but over time, it becomes clear that he is the active party and the master a mere appetite.

Marx, too, was frustrated with the radical students and intellectuals of his day in the German universities. While they endlessly fought out the differences between the Conservative Hegelians, the Young Hegelians and the Feuerbachians, Marx said that these antitheses would never be overcome by thought alone, but through practice, whereby the differences would cease to be hardened divisions, and settle back into being different facets of the same problem.

It was the transcendent principle that allowed the resolution of the debates. But the transcendent principle is exactly what is taken out today. The resurrection of Hegel in France in the mid-twentieth century dismissed the centrality of *Geist*, or Spirit, as a retrograde and unimportant aspect of the much more interesting dialectic of self and other. But they had forgotten Marx's advice that it is precisely in the apparently mystified form of spirit that the historical transience of Hegel lay. Removing Spirit left Hegel's philosophy as one of a perpetual cycle of opposition between Self and Other.

This is what the American Critical Race theorist Kimberlé Crenshaw's intersectionality achieves – much the same as the intersubjectivity of the French post-Hegelians. Transcendence of division is not possible, only what the Human Resources department calls the 'management of diversity' or the Romans called 'divide and rule'.

Really I should stop there, but there is one last step I want to make, which is probably a mistake, and that is to look at the questions of social justice that the intersectionalists talk about. I say that it is a mistake because I do not really believe that the ideas we are looking at are remotely connected to any concept of social justice, they are instead primarily debate-things among satisfied elites.

A lot has changed in the relations of men to women, and of the races – or to be clearer about it, in the social reproduction process that gave those identities salience. The call-out culture that has become symptomatic of today's campaigns for social justice is incapable of a measured account of reality, because it is purely logical, not theoretical. Simply because a subject position can be articulated it attains reality. Reducing oppression to a logical structure of 'othering', as innumerable undergraduate essays do, means that any instance of judgment or discrimination can be made equivalent to white supremacy.

So, for example, a great deal of time and attention has been given over to the position of transgendered individuals, both on campus and off. Now, any lively social movement ought to have a wide degree of tolerance for people's personal behaviours. But intolerance towards the transgendered is not a social problem – however much it might present a specific problem for the transgendered. Around my daughter's school there are posters for a campaign fronted by the Genderbread Man. There are no transgender children at the school. There are precious few who are gay. The demand that the transgendered be recognised as women (or men) elevates a logical position above reality itself. A man who aspires to be a woman is still a man who aspires to be a woman.

The old order, in which the elite forged a national consensus around race is much less important than it was. So too the gendered division of labour, in which women were primarily preoccupied with unpaid domestic work is of diminishing importance. More women in the workplace, and less dependency upon the male breadwinner represents a substantial change. Yet most debate about race and gender talks about these things as if we were still living under the ancient conditions of white supremacy and patriarchy. Preoccupied with division they are blind to the much-reported coalescence of social attitudes, and social experiences. The critique of the old order drives towards the creation of a new order, in which human relations are heavily problematised. But that is much harder to characterise. Critiquing the new order sometimes sounds like a defence of the old order, but that is not really a problem.

The ad hominem rule is a good one. Its real foundation is the ambition that reason should stand above experience. It is hard to sustain because reason has been pulled down off its pedestal. In the modern world the 'wise wound' insists that you STFU, sit down, and listen. At its most destructive, it leads to the banning of speakers at universities, the withdrawal of difficult texts, and the corrosive pressure to police one's thoughts and opinions to make them acceptable. It is true that there is an irreducible experience that cannot be shared. But it is the least interesting truth. It is what the phenomenological method enshrines as 'the things themselves'. They seem so authentic, like the bent stick in the water. But they are not true. Only reason, working on experience, brings you truth.

References

Crenshaw, K. (2015) *On Intersectionality: The Essential Writings of Kimberlé Crenshaw.* New York: The New Press.

Emerson, R. W. (1860) *Worship.* Available at: http://www.bartleby.com/5/117.html (accessed 31/03/16).

Fraser, N. (2013) 'How feminism became capitalism's handmaiden - and how to reclaim it' in *The Guardian* (14/10/13). Available at: http://www.theguardian.com/commentisfree/2013/oct/14/feminism-capitalist-handmaiden-neoliberal (accessed 05/01/16).

Laing, R. D. (1971) *Knots.* London: Penguin Books.

Lowe, P. and Jonson, A. (1998) 'There is No Such Thing as Free Speech: An Interview with Stanley Fish'. Available at: http://australianhumanitiesreview.org/archive/Issue-February-1998/fish.html (01/02/98) (accessed 05/01/16).

MacKinnon, C. (1993) *Only Words.* Cambridge, MA: Harvard University Press.

MacKinnon, C. (1989) *Towards a Feminist Theory of the State.* Cambridge MA: Harvard University Press.

Pollitt, K. (2015) 'Feminism Needs More Speakers Who Aren't Right 100 Per Cent of the Time' in *The Nation* (05/11/15). Available at: http://www.thenation.com/article/feminism-needs-more-thinkers-who-arent-right-100-per cent-of-the-time/ (accessed 05/01/16).

Rorty, R. (1989) *Contingency, Irony and Solidarity.* Cambridge: Cambridge University Press.

Smith, E. (2015) 'By Whatever Means Necessary: The Origins of the "No Platform" Policy'. Available at: https://hatfulofhistory.wordpress.com/2015/11/03/by-whatever-means-necessary-the-origins-of-the-no-platform-policy/ (accessed 05/01/16).

Solnit, R. (2014) *Men Explain Things to Me*. Chicago: Haymarket Books.

Part Two

The University in the Twenty-First Century

On Academic and Other Freedoms

Thomas Docherty

Why should the issue of academic freedom be of interest to anyone other than an academic? For most people, the idea of being able, as a paid employee, to criticise the conditions of knowledge and normative modes of behaviour in one's institution will seem perverse. As Stanley Fish puts it: 'Why should members of a particular profession be granted latitudes and exemptions not enjoyed by other citizens? Why, for example, should college and university professors be free to criticise their superiors when employees in other workplaces might face discipline or dismissal?' (Fish, 2014, p. 1).

For many of those other citizens, the cries that academic freedom is under threat might well be met with 'and so it should be'. Employees everywhere might like the idea of being able, with impunity, to criticise freely their conditions, or the general state of worldly affairs, or their boss without fear of jeopardising their position. Indeed, it is a fairly safe hypothesis that, for most citizens, academic freedom might well look like the icing on the already extremely privileged cake that is being enjoyed by well-paid and comfortable employees in our universities.

Against this, we have the very clear historical statement that university professors are, indeed, exceptions in some way to the general rules governing employment. One of the earliest formal investigations into the nature of academic freedom is to be found in the 1915 *Declaration of Principles on Academic Freedom and Academic Tenure* laid out by the American Association of University Professors (AAUP). There, we find the constitutional claim that, in fact, professors are not 'employees' at all.

Precisely one century on, this document raises a number of key issues that are increasingly pertinent in our own contemporary situation. The AAUP document makes a distinction between what it calls 'proprietary' colleges 'designed for the propagation of specific doctrines prescribed by those who have furnished its endowment', (1915, p. 292) and other 'ordinary' colleges. 'Proprietary institutions' – which in 1915 meant primarily religious institutions, described as 'instruments of propaganda' acting 'in the interests of the religious faith professed by the church or denomination creating it' (1915, p. 293) – were becoming increasingly rare by 1915. Where they exist, however, the AAUP *Declaration* indicates that their Trustees 'have a right to demand that everything be subordinated' to the specific ends of the propaganda required by those Trustees (1915, p. 293).

'Ordinary' public institutions are not governed by proprietary interests, and therefore constitute 'a public trust'. The logic then follows that those who manage such institutions have no moral rights over the activities of their professors. Indeed, 'All claim to such right is waived by the appeal to the general public for contributions and for moral support in the maintenance, not of a propaganda, but of a non-partisan institution of learning' (AAUP, 1915, p. 293). Any institution, then, that imposes such restrictions upon its professors is, ipso facto, in breach of public trust, and has effectively if surreptitiously converted itself into a proprietary institution.

According to the *Declaration*, professors in our regular university sector are not, in the strict sense, employees of their institution, even if they are appointees within that institution. Their responsibilities are not to their boss or line-manager, nor are they even to their institution as such; rather, the key moral responsibility is to the public. Further, that responsibility is realised in the professor's relation to 'purely scientific and educational questions' (AAUP, 1915, p. 295).

Today, however, public institutions worldwide are increasingly determined by the principles of privatisation or of 'proprietary interest'. The situation is exacerbated further when the 'proprietary interest' in question is a fully political interest, governed by the logic of privatisation as such. The consequence of such privatisation is that university management and leadership now arrogates to itself the kinds of control over academic freedom that are more appropriate to an institution designed for the propagation of a doctrine. Structurally, the circumscription and limitation of academic freedom converts the university – and its professors – into instruments for the propaganda of privatisation as such.

In his detailed study of the UK's political programme of the last half century, including the privatisation of mail, rail, utilities and housing, James Meek provides the figures to show what this means. The process of 'meta-privatisation' has been a success: 'it put more money into the hands of a small number of the very wealthiest people, at the expense of the elderly, the sick, the jobless and the working poor' (Meek, 2014, p. 21).

Meek follows through the logic of the political economics of privatisation, and arrives at a somewhat shocking conclusion. As he points out, we tend to think of taxation as something that involves government directly. However, 'If a payment to an authority, public or private, is compulsory, it's a tax' (Meek, 2014, p. 21). After all, if we cannot do without electricity, then 'the electricity bill is an electricity tax'. The same goes for water, say; and for rail for those who must use the railways. Given the UK's new tuition fee structure, 'students pay the university tax'.

The shocking result of this general set of propositions is that 'meta-privatisation is the privatisation of the tax system itself; even, it could be said, the privatisation of us, the former citizens of Britain' (Meek, 2014, p. 22). This contemporary predicament is essentially endorsed by a managerialist structure in our university institutions that demands fealty to brand instead of responsibility towards knowledge for the sake of the general public or taxpayer.

The university institution, in the UK as elsewhere, is increasingly a 'proprietary institution'; and this means that professors are being systematically perverted in their duties by managements that have either forgotten their moral duty to the public, or are expressly determined to corrupt their institution. The demands of maintaining the 'university brand' is symptomatic of this; and, in a series of increasingly brazen moves, institutions worldwide are not just protecting their brand, but branding professors as 'their' human resource, their 'employees', requiring – in extreme examples – that they even adopt an approved 'tone of voice' for public engagements or communications (see Newey, 2015 and also comments by Mehdi Alioua, 2015 on what he calls the *dictature des moeurs*'). This represents a systematic attack on the responsibility of the professor; and, with it, a systematic attack on the very idea of citizenship and the university's relation to the public sphere.

Given these conditions, I will argue that academic freedom is not at all a privilege. On the contrary, it is a very founding condition of the possibility of an academic doing her or his job at all. It is more than a right: it is a fundamental necessity, a prerequisite for being an academic. Further, my claim is that this is of interest not just 'within' the walls of the academy; rather, academic freedom is the founding condition of the possibility of social freedom as such. It is that important, and therefore of interest to a general public.

It is not simply an issue of governance; nor is it simply an issue of having the freedom to 'speak out' against institutional injustices or failings. It is what makes us – and our institutions – socially responsible; and it should be – must be – the cornerstone of the very existence of our institutions.

The fact that academic freedom exists only in the pious mouthing of regulatory protocols that are easily circumvented or ignored is the real scandal facing the higher education establishment today. That scandal helps explain the general demise of democratic participation in the formation and constitutions of our societies, our living together in free assembly.

The attack on academic freedom, therefore, is an attack on the freedom of people other than academics. Academics are simply the visible collateral damage in a yet more insidious attack on democracy and justice.

The attack is the vanguard action of a system in which the substantially privileged – who are not the academic community, but precisely those very wealthy individuals, beneficiaries of the privatisation project referred to by James Meek – maintain their privileges and seek to extend further their own wealth, at the cost of others less privileged. The construction of the image of the academic as privileged is itself a method of diverting attention from the real source of social privilege, which remains class-based and wealth-based.

To defend academic freedom, in these conditions, is to defend democracy, justice and freedom more widely. The sequential logic of my case is laid out in three stages: first, the exploration of how thinking itself is increasingly restricted; second, how free speech is endangered; third, how this leads to a near-criminalisation of free assembly, of communication and thinking-together.

I start from the ostensibly weakest, yet most 'professional', account of academic freedom: the idea that it is the freedom to say whatever one finds to be the case within one's disciplinary domain. Stanley Fish calls this the 'It's Just a Job' school of academic freedom. This account presents the academic institution as broadly equivalent to a medieval guild: it is autonomous in the sense that its practitioners determine its practices, and give legitimacy (or not) to specific actions within its own purview. The practitioners determine their own constitution, in all senses. They determine who can be a member; and the members determine what passes as appropriate and proper action of the institution or guild as such.

This has the attraction of being a modest claim, governed by purely professional interests that serve to respect and even to guarantee guild-autonomy in its fullest sense. However, it quickly runs into the buffers of failed definitions. What are the limits of my discipline? How are they defined? Fish holds that these are consensually agreed by the community of academics already within and constituting my discipline. Yet that is, in the first place, a circular argument: I become a member of the guild by agreeing to the consensual frameworks of the guild's self-descriptions, and these, in circular turn, are what legitimise my membership in the first place. This is not autonomy; it is a closed-shop mentality, rooted in the refusal to answer to critical scrutiny from those outside the guild. It is governed by the logic of atomisation: to every profession its own closed private space; to every constituent her own private office, doors closed against the world.

Against this, I hold that thinking, as such, knows and should acknowledge no disciplinary boundary whatsoever. Thinking – as opposed to mere repetition of received ideas – is *what happens* when we are jolted into a perception that could not have been predicted by the established norms of our discipline. This is close to what Jacques Derrida meant when he wrote of 'the university without condition', in which there should be 'an *unconditional* freedom to question and assert, or even, going still further, the right to say publicly all that is required by research, knowledge, and thought concerning the *truth*' (Derrida, 2002, p. 202). In this suspension of conditionality (or suspending of restrictive conditions), research, knowledge and thought are all governed precisely by the breaking or disruption of condition as such. The activity of thinking – and its correlatives of teaching and research – exists precisely when one goes beyond what the disciplinary boundary legitimises as normative. Thinking is of the nature of a material event.

Respect for and repetition or consolidation of the norms of one's discipline is actually nothing more or less than accounting. The professor becomes what the French system calls an *agrégé-répétiteur*, whose role is to repeat and require the student to repeat in turn what passes traditionally for accepted truth and knowledge within a discipline. Autonomy here is reduced to self-propagating self-assurance and self-promotion. This is the very definition of privilege as such: the maintenance of a system – like a class-system, say - that one refuses to subject to scrutiny or criticism. Such privilege knows no possibility of thought; and criticism – especially in its form as freethinking, thinking unconstrained and 'without condition' – is its anathema.

We can counter Fish's extremely limiting idea of academic freedom with an example. At the start of Shakespeare's *King Lear*, the king divides the kingdom, and shares its constituent elements among his three daughters. In understanding this scene, we need knowledge beyond the basics of understanding the semantic content of the words as they are spoken around 1600 and since. That knowledge does not come from within 'English literature', but from different disciplinary fields. For example, one of the reasons for the gathering of nobles at the court is that Lear is about to settle the dowry of Cordelia, with two rival suitors (Burgundy and France) in the wings. The disciplines of history and politics make sense of the distinction between those two figures. 'History' or 'anthropology' yield knowledge of the systems of kinship and property relations, especially in the field of international relations and politics that are shaped by marriage. It is not the case that marriage, as we now know it (based largely on what Lawrence Stone once called 'affective individualism' (Stone, 1977)), was always normative. Indeed, for many even at the time of Shakespeare's writing of this scene, it would have been unusual; and this knowledge allows us to understand more fully Cordelia's feistiness in the opening scene (for a fuller analysis see Docherty, 1987). History, sociology, anthropology are all involved here, in 'Eng. Lit'.

To what extent is our understanding of *King Lear* – that apotheosis of 'English literature' – governed by the protocols of the guild? And suppose I try to stage this play now (and any reading of the text is, of course, such a contemporary re-staging), in the wake of the referendum on Scottish independence of 2014, say: is there a contemporary relevance in the idea of splitting up 'the nation' even though 'the nation' of which Shakespeare wrote did not include Scotland in precisely the same legal ways that it now does? Can we avoid the undisciplined thinking that brings contemporary political debate to bear on the text and our reading?

Fish's modestly limited position is abstract, reduced to the point of meaninglessness before concrete example. It is simply impossible that when I walk through the doors of my institution, I cede my citizenship of the world and become 'the professor'. It is yet more impossible that, when I open the pages of *King Lear*, I become 'the professor of *King Lear* studies, Act 1 scene 1 line 1' and so on. There is an atomisation of the intellect here structurally occluding the fact that to think at all requires, fundamentally, that we disallow intellectual boundaries.

This is also the reason why many university managements prefer Fish's position. The existing structures and protocols governing academic freedom in our institutions are not only restricted, but also restrictive. Our academic activities are being thereby systematically perverted, through a more general process of atomisation – such as we see in Fish's preferred 'Professional/It's Just a Job' position – and its political corollary or underpinning in privatisation.

Academic freedom in thinking, then, cannot be circumscribed by disciplinary boundaries. Now, let us examine the very idea of disciplines – and indeed of discipline as such.

The organisation of knowledge into disciplines serves numerous functions. It can be an administrative convenience, allowing for the distribution of budgets, allocation of facilities, and the like. It can also be a way of determining modes of thought: the mode of thinking required for working in a chemistry laboratory, we might say, is not necessarily like that required for work in French language and literature. That is: disciplines establish protocols for academic behaviour, and they can be used to structure and police that behaviour. This is the logical corollary of Fish's guild-structure. More significantly, though, disciplines produce disciples, followers, within a structural hierarchy of charismatic 'leaderships'. The clearest example of this occurs within religions, which are themselves sometimes the respectable cover for unpalatable political positions.

This raises the question of how academic freedom interacts with institutional governance; and, in particular, how issues of governance related to behaviour impinge upon our free thinking (as above) and also, now, our free speaking. Disciplining the tongue – our modes of speech – becomes central; and it relates to how leaders govern and manage institutions and the activities of individuals within those institutions.

We typically encourage discipline in the making of an argument or in the explication of scientific experiment. It helps keep our work intellectually focused, gives it a shape and purpose, and allows for a judgement to be passed upon its cogency or coherence. In this sense, discipline is central to argumentative value. This comes close to saying that *how we express* our thought is as important as the substance of that thought. Yet what we see happening now is that dissident thinking – thinking as such, we might say – is being deemed illegitimate unless it conforms to modes of speech that are validated by our leadership and by the disciplinary value they place on our *behaviour*, behaviour that we now say has to exemplify 'the brand'. In short, what we witness here is an extension of 'discipline' into its punishment mode, in which our freedom to speak as we wish becomes subject to policed surveillance, under the guise of conforming to the brand or to the image of the institution, as expressed by our management and leadership.

Perhaps the most egregious instances of discipline such as this coming into play have been in the US, where many professors are now finding themselves constrained by 'Title IX' provisions of the US Department of Education Office for Civil Rights. Title IX protects people against sexual discrimination and harassment. Increasingly, however, it is being used in a way that collapses the distinction between speech and action, such that speech *about* sexual discrimination is being described as if it constitutes an *act* of sexual discrimination as such. The consequence is that freely expressing a view – any view – about matters pertaining to sex, becomes intrinsically damaging to the speaker. The audience may, at some unspecified time and/or place decide that what she or he has heard upsets their intellectual equilibrium; and they can therefore claim to have been harassed by the statement. One especially egregious example is the case of Laura Kipnis, Professor of Film Studies at Northwestern University (Kipnis, 29/05/15). And, as with sex, so also with any and all other forms of discrimination. The consequence is that *nothing at all* can ever be a topic for free discussion in which the speaker is not jeopardising her or his future, her or his standing.

The logical corollary is startling. It means that, for example, we cannot any longer discuss *Hard Times*, say, in case anyone identifying with 'the poor', say, feels that the representation of poor people therein is less than 100 per cent positive. They may declare themselves harassed or victimised by the mere fact of a teacher asking them to read the text without having issued a so-called 'trigger warning'. Similarly, with any literary text that engages issues of sexual identity, race, gender, class, age, nation or any other concept around which a political identity may be built (which is quite a lot of literature). This is not even to start on the laboratory sciences, where genetics or artificial intelligence or virtually any other scientific activity might cause intellectual upset.

The result is that controversy – engaged speech as such – is eliminated from the institution. Further, not only is controversy eliminated, but so also is anything that might be identified as a cause of political unhappiness. If I effectively bar us from reading *Hard Times*, say (or if I ensure that, in reading it, we will all feel 'safe' because nothing controversial will ever be allowed to enter the discussion), I am ensuring that less time can be given to thinking about the existence of the poor in nineteenth-century literature and culture. I eliminate poverty from social and political consideration. The point of this is to ensure that students and other citizens accept the world as they find it, and give up on any belief that by thinking and talking about problems we might actually change things. What happens in the classroom stays within the classroom; and, crucially, no event of thinking is to be allowed expression in that room, lest someone gets upset now or later.

There is a conflation here of free speech with action. University administration runs a mile from confronting this, for fear of lawsuits and – essentially – for fear of being taken to court for upsetting those private 'customers' of our proprietary brand, formerly known as 'students'.

Universities, it is asserted, need to be 'safe spaces'. While this once meant that they should be spaces in which one was able to think unusual or dissident thoughts without fear of jeopardising one's position and livelihood, now it is increasingly taken to mean that they should be spaces in which no one is ever threatened by thinking at all, especially if thinking might force one to reconsider one's already settled values. How would we, now, ever, read Rilke's poem 'On the archaic torso of Apollo' where, standing before that torso, *'da ist keine Stelle / die dich nicht sieht. Du mußt dein Leben ändern'*: 'there is no place / that does not see you. You must change your life' (see Rilke, 2011, pp. 80–81).

Art, by definition, is not a 'safe space', for it provokes thinking and, worse, the requirement that we assume the responsibility of our freedom. It is this – freedom – that causes such anguish, for it means we must determine and be responsible for our own behaviour. In our time, however, the norms of our proper behaviour are, as it were, 'outsourced' to formalised and managed protocols; and we find ourselves no longer responsible for anything, but accountable for everything. Such a position is one that reduces the possibility of *both* free speech *and* free action.

Yet, you might say, how can this be so in an age when universities everywhere vaunt interdisciplinarity, and where university managements themselves claim that disciplinary thinking is too restrictive? The response is clear. Once interdisciplinarity is normative, research structures are challenged. The question becomes how we establish priorities for research and for differential funding. Where we once had a 'conflict of the faculties' (a two-cultures debate between academic disciplines), we now have something entirely different (STEM against the rest). Governments now arrogate to themselves the right to determine national research priorities; funding agencies (like Research Councils) then follow that lead; and university managers internalise it within institutions. Research itself is no longer based in the free exercise of thought and speech; rather, it is 'governed', and governed primarily by financial, monetary and economic interests.

Indirectly, we become precisely the unacknowledged 'proprietary institution' in which, as the 1915 *Declaration* indicated, we are servants and employees of our proprietary masters, instruments now of governmental propaganda. Thus, if the government determines that 'ageing', say, is a priority, then our academic work has to be cast under that sign, if it is to have any substantive existence – no matter our own intellectual demands or moral responsibilities. The result is a corrupting of research itself.

Contemporary interdisciplinarity leads also to the elimination of disciplinary departments, and their replacement with interdisciplinary 'schools' and 'colleges' (of arts/sciences and so on). This weakens disciplinary solidarity, further atomising the institution. Within 'school' or 'college', collective identities are fractured, and colleagues are increasingly isolated, their only real relation being one of competition and rivalry for funds and institutional prestige.

The result? We weaken and de-naturalise the free assembly of speakers – which might, of course, pass as a perfect description of what a university should be. General freedom of assembly is under threat, as a direct consequence of the weakness of our ideas of academic freedom. The institution replicates the 'proprietary society', the privatisation of our social being, where our only relation is one of competitive individualism. Yet, if there is no free assembly, based upon free speech which in turn is grounded in the freedom to think in a dissident fashion, then it follows that, as Mrs. Thatcher once put it, 'there is no such thing as society'. If this is the case, then there can be no democracy either, and no just judgements (or justice) based on the free expression of freely thought propositions. Society becomes the conformist crowd, following the charismatic leader, no questions asked.

Do we want this? Do we want the corollary of utter conformism to be proprietary interest, especially in its politicised form of acquisitive and competitive individualism? Some people do seem to want this. It is a matter of enormous and grave concern that some of them are running universities.

References

American Association of University Professors. (1915) *Declaration of Principles*. Available at: http://www.aaup.org/NR/rdonlyres/A6520A9D-0A9A-47B3-B550-C006B5B224E7/0/1915Declaration.pdf (accessed 31/03/16).

Alioua, M. (2015) 'Maroc: "On est loin de Mai 68, mais ça se prépare!"' in *Nouvel Obs*. Available at: http://tempsreel.nouvelobs.com/monde/20150707.OBS2271/maroc-on-est-loin-de-mai-68-mais-ca-se-prepare.html?xtor=RSS-19 (accessed 28/10/15).

Derrida, J. (2002) *Without Alibi*. (Kamuf, P. ed. and trans.) Stanford: Stanford University Press.

Docherty, T. (1987) *On Modern Authority: The Theory and Condition of Writing 1500 to the Present Day*. Sussex: Harvester Press.

Fish, S. (2014) *Versions of Academic Freedom*. Chicago: University of Chicago Press.

Kipnis, L. (2015) 'My Title IX Inquisition' in *The Chronicle of Higher Education*. (29/05/15). Available at: http://laurakipnis.com/wp-content/uploads/2010/08/My-Title-IX-Inquisition-The-Chronicle-Review-.pdf (accessed 28/10/15).

Meek, J. (2014) *Private Island*. London: Verso Books.,

Newey, G. (2015) 'Mind Your Tone' in *London Review of Books* blog (10/04/15). Available at: http://www.lrb.co.uk/blog/2015/04/10/glen-newey/mind-your-tone/ (accessed 28/10/15).

Rilke, R. M. (2011 [1908]) 'On the archaic torso of Apollo', (in Ranson, S. and Sutherland M. trans.) *Selected Poems with parallel German text*. Oxford: Oxford University Press.

Stone, L. (1977) *The Family, Sex and Marriage in England, 1500-1800*. London: Penguin.

Faith in the Academy: Religion at University

Rania Hafez

Recently universities have found themselves torn between upholding values of academic freedom, of free speech and expression on campus, and pandering to a new orthodoxy that defines students as vulnerable adults and likely to be 'damaged' by contrary opinions. This has been most marked when it comes to issues of faith and students' religious identity and beliefs. This chapter considers the contradictory position universities find themselves in, on one hand seeking to protect students' religious sensibilities by sanctioning illiberal practices and restricting criticism, and on the other seeking to limit freedom of expression by banning certain faith speakers in the fear they will 'radicalise' vulnerable students. It will reflect on the troubled relationship between religion and the academy, especially as the current government seeks to conscript universities and their staff in surveillance over the thoughts and leanings of their students. This is not simply a case of academic freedom under attack; it is more fundamental and far reaching. The current troubled relationship between religion and universities is a manifestation of something far more serious: that we as a society have lost faith in the academy.

Religion in the academy

Religion might have an ambivalent presence on university campuses nowadays but faith and the academic tradition have a long history. From the medieval monasteries of Europe that instituted the education of monks and priests to the heyday of Islamic scholarship that saw the establishment of Baghdad's House of Wisdom (Lyons, 2009), Christianity and Islam both acted as catalysts in transmitting ancient philosophical traditions and building on them. It was in the interface between theology and rational enquiry that academic scholarship thrived.

The subsequent separation between religion and the university could be seen as the inevitable result of empirical rationality and the ascent of scientific enquiry. Religion lost its important place in the academy becoming either a purely personal matter or a subject for study in theology degrees (Wuthnow, 2007). However, the continuing divide between faith as represented by religion and reason as represented by the academy is not simply a matter of secularism taking over from belief. It has more to do with social and political shifts than with a natural antipathy between science and religion. These days it is common to see frequent headlines linking religion with universities, not because religious scholarship is adding to the wealth of their intellectual capital, but because religion is seen as an insidious interloper posing real threats to the academy and its intellectual freedoms.

The ambiguous role religion has come to play in the life of the academy came about initially as universities sought to accommodate an increasingly multi-cultural student body. Along with other Muslim students in the

1980s, I lobbied my university for prayer facilities. The request was for purely practical needs, a space where we could conduct our daily and Friday prayers. We were helped by the ascendance of multicultural awareness and policies. In time religious societies proliferated and it is now common to find prayer rooms in almost all campuses.

But that welcome accommodation of students' religious requirements soon became an acceptance and subsequently an endorsement of illiberal practices. The gender segregation within religious observance eventually crossed the threshold of the prayer room into the seminar room. Functions and talks organised by some religious societies required gender segregated seating. This was rarely challenged, and when it was, universities justified allowing such practices out of respect for the students' identity and beliefs. The ascendance of identity politics and the fear of being branded racist were the main drivers behind an almost unquestioning acceptance of almost any behaviour that students claimed was a manifestation of their religious identity, however spurious that claim.

Religion and the undermining of academic freedom

Cultural essentialism has thus become one of the orthodoxies that has permeated contemporary universities in the UK. It means that students see it as their right to reject any idea they deem contrary to their faith, and feel justified in doing so. In this ubiquitous therapeutic culture that brands students as vulnerable and in need of protection from potential offence, the emotional and personal has taken precedence over the intellectual. This is not restricted to the policies for student satisfaction but has filtered down to the very pedagogy of higher education where our teaching is meant to entertain rather than challenge students and where we must issue trigger warnings lest the content of our lectures causes them undue distress. Students are already primed from university marketing and induction material to expect their views to hold sway and that the function of all who work at the university is to meet their needs. Nowhere are the new recruits inducted into the concept and practice of academic freedom. We tell them we will listen to their voice when they speak but rarely teach them that they must allow others the same freedom.

When it comes to universities, the relationship between lecturers and students, the content of what is taught and how, and even the administrative running of the institution, are all now defined by policy edicts and subject to regulation. Nowhere is state encroachment more demarcated than with the issue of religion on campus. If religion poses any threat to academic freedom it is in two ways, both external to religion but exemplified by these two statements: 'You can't say that, it offends me' and 'You can't say that, it's dangerous.'

As students' cultural identities and their 'voice' becomes paramount and unassailable within universities, they have increasingly come to see their views as taking precedence over academic principles including academic freedom. This is especially true when these views can be justified with recourse to the label of religious belief. Even scientific knowledge and facts are subject to the belief test. In a widely-reported incident in November 2011 over one hundred university students, some of them medics, walked out of a lecture on evolution at University College London (*Daily Mail*, 28/11/11). They claimed that the teaching of evolution contradicted their faith and asserted their right not to be taught it.

The story and the reaction to it illustrate how faith in the academy as a place for engaging in a battle of all ideas is being undermined. The students felt that the ideas presented, regardless of the fact that they are based on empirical science, challenged their 'protected' view of the world. They displayed a sense of entitlement not emanating from their faith, but rather from an approach to multiculturalism, broadly espoused and often promoted by government. This approach elevates personal identity over rational thinking. The students found evolution 'offensive' so did what our society tells them they are entitled to do. They refused to listen and by their refusal they were seeking to 'silence' their lecturers.

This censorship of ideas and views is not confined to students of faith. The mere anticipation of potential offence can lead the university to self-censor even before anything has been said or done. A prime example is the recent refusal by Warwick University's students' union to host an atheist speaker, Maryam Namazie, who is well-known for her anti-Islam views. Namazie had been invited to speak by the Warwick Atheists, Secularists and Humanists society when the Students' Union moved to block the event. They justified their action by stating that they had 'a duty of care to conduct a risk assessment for each speaker who wishes to come to campus'. (Adams, 29/09/15) They went on to say that because some articles written both by Namazie and about her indicate that 'she is highly inflammatory, and could incite hatred on campus' they felt they had to ban her. They declared that their decision was taken 'in deference to the right of Muslim students not to feel intimidated or discriminated against on their university campus... rather than in the interests of suppressing free speech or freedom of expression' (Adams, 29/09/15). It seems that all Maryam Namazie was guilty of was espousing secular views that challenged Islam and this was enough to have her banned. The irony is that members of the students' union overlooked the fact that their own censorious action treated their Muslim members as too vulnerable to cope with contrary opinions. By banning Namazie, the union in effect discriminated against Muslims, and indeed all students. Moreover, by claiming to protect freedom of expression they essentially ended it.

The way religious practice and identity are manifest on campus illustrates the intellectual insecurity that is taking hold of the academy in favour of new political orthodoxies. In their eagerness to embrace the new politics that pander to cultural identity, however tenuous, universities find themselves allowing curbs on freedom of speech and sanctioning discriminatory practices that would be unacceptable in other contexts. Yet the justification is simple and much rehearsed, both on campus and outside in wider society: 'You can't say that, it offends my beliefs.'

The retrenchment of intellectual confidence and authority permeates the academy and manifests itself unsurprisingly in the behaviour of students and students' unions up and down the country. Students walk out on lectures they consider contrary to their religious beliefs and students' unions 'no platform' speakers who represent views that are contrary to current orthodoxies, whether to do with faith, gender or culture.

It would be a mistake to blame religion for these illiberal practices. Rather, it is confusion about the academy's fundamental role of fostering academic freedom and intellectual rigour that is at the heart of the problem. When the students walked out of that scientific lecture, some commentators saw it as evidence of too much freedom on campus. Newspapers such as the *Daily Mail* and websites such as *Jihad Watch* claimed it was yet another aspect of the Islamic extremism that had been allowed to take root on university campuses across the country. These commentators blamed universities themselves for encouraging it. They called for universities to further curtail academic freedom – of Islamic societies and Muslim students in particular. Even before the dubious Prevent Duty made suspects out of students, academic freedom was under threat from those who fear ideas and would rather silence certain voices.

Preventing academic freedom

Perhaps the most pertinent of current religiously-inspired threats to academic freedom is the Prevent Duty and its requirement that universities should police the behaviour, opinion, and even personal inclinations of its students. An impossible feat let alone an ethical one, and one that does not just pose a risk to academic freedom but also to fundamental civil liberties of thought and association. Full details of the Prevent Duty are covered in another chapter in more detail, but I would like to address the way religion and the academy have been put at loggerheads through such a misguided policy.

The most glaring inconsistency in the Prevent Duty and associated anti-radicalisation policies is that neither the terms 'extremism' nor 'radicalisation' have been defined satisfactorily. If we look at government guidance around the subject, we find the terms used so loosely that universities are at a loss as to how to interpret them. At Staffordshire University, a postgraduate student quietly reading a library book in the university's library was questioned and reported to security guards as a potential extremist. The fact that he is studying for an MA in Terrorism, Crime and Global Security and was reading one of the course textbooks did not seem enough to exonerate him. The university subsequently apologised to the student and admitted fault, claiming it was responding to a 'very broad duty ... to have due regard to the need to prevent people from being drawn into terrorism'. The university also conceded that the duty was 'underpinned by guidance ... [that] contains insufficient detail to provide clear practical direction in an environment such as the university's' (Ramesh and Halliday, 24/09/15). The blame is properly laid at the door of government regulation, although the question that begs itself is why universities did not oppose such policies in the first place?

The issue here is not simply one of insufficient guidance, but rather the erroneous link between radicalisation and universities. The fact is there is no evidence that UK universities or even universities' Islamic societies, however 'conservative' the views they may hold, are places where terrorism or terrorist acts have been initiated or planned. And the incident at Staffordshire University is not the only one of its kind. There have been similar instances where lecturers and researchers have been detained and in some cases lost their employment because of routine academic activity. The well-known case of Nottingham University's

Hicham Yezza and Rizwan Sabir in 2008 provides a germane example. Rizwan, then a PhD student, had shared with Hicham an electronic document known as 'The Al-Qaida Training Manual'. The document, not actually created by Al-Qaeda, was readily available online. Both men were arrested and held for several days and although all charges were eventually dropped, the series of events had a profound effect on both the researchers and other academics. The policy encourages caution and self-censorship.

Rizwan Sabir has since become a lecturer specialising in counter-terrorism. In an email interview conducted for this chapter, I asked him what he thought was the impact of current anti-terror policies on academic freedom. He told me that: 'With the embedding of Prevent into the education and university sectors through the Counter-Terrorism and Security Act 2015, it is fair to say things are getting worse for students and staff. In the past, the police were responsible for investigating and apprehending individuals suspected of being involved in terrorism. Now, however, this responsibility has been outsourced to university lectures and administrative staff who are not accountable in the same way.' He outlined how this can lead to censorship of research material: 'The fear of being subjected to coercive measures is leading individuals and organisations – such as the British Library which has refused to hold Taliban documents – to self-censor. It is undeniable that the consequences of deeply draconian measures are having highly damaging consequences for academics, researchers and students.'

Another feature of this febrile atmosphere around religion in universities is the rush to make spurious connections between terrorists and their alma maters. For example, the accusation that individuals like

Michael Adebolajo, one of the murderers of Fusilier Lee Rigby, or Mohammed Emwazi, the ISIS fighter known as 'Jihadi John', were 'radicalised' by contact with dangerous dogma at university is tenuous at best. It puts immense pressure on universities. They are expected to spot and stop the development of extreme ideas in their students and universities are given the near-impossible task of trying to ascertain the mental dispositions of their students and then intervene to 'correct' it. Worse, it has created an underlying air of suspicion between staff and students. At the beginning of this academic year one of my second-year Muslim students seemed to be sporting a slightly longer and bushier beard than last year. I found myself wondering whether it was a hipster beard or a sign of radicalisation! It also occurred to me that in this atmosphere of doubt, it would be problematic for me to engage my students in debates around religion as they may fear being accused of extremism and I would fear accusations of radicalising my own students.

The case for faith in the academy

And so it is that religion and the academy find themselves locked in conflict, though not necessarily conflict of their own making. With the decline of religion as an intellectual endeavour, and of revolutionary ideologies in influencing politics, the modern state has eschewed the goal of social transformation in favour of technocratic management (Malik, 21/09/15). What we have ended up with is a pseudo-religious discourse of good and evil coupled with a banal utilitarian and instrumentalist approach to constrict the freedom of the academy. Ostensibly a forum for discussion, delineation and discernment, the university now finds itself stripped of its basic function to exercise intellectual and ethical judgement. And religion is reduced to either a state of emotional vulnerability or a vehicle for violent extremism. It is vital that we not only expose the threats to academic freedom that are posed by this view of faith but that we advocate actively for faith in religion and faith in the academy, as well as freedom for both.

We will need to answer some questions such as 'what good is the academy?' and 'what good is religion?' To begin to answer these questions, we need to recognise that both should allow the space for meaning and sentiment to flourish, rather than reducing all questions to utilitarian purposes. At best, they are both open communities of enquiry that deal with ideas and ideals that can encapsulate the best of humanity.

The whole point about faith is to assert personal confidence in impossible things. Having faith in the academy is to have confidence in human intellect and reason and the centrality of freedom of ideas. It is also the space where we examine and challenge orthodoxies and propose alternatives. Back in 1969, Isaiah Berlin avowed his concern that academics and thinkers were failing to challenge dangerous ideas and warned of the consequences of this failure:

> There has, perhaps, been no time in modern history when so large a number of human beings, in both the East and the West, have had their notions, and indeed their lives, so deeply altered, and in some cases violently upset, by fanatically held social and political doctrines. Dangerous, because when ideas are neglected by those who ought to attend to them – that is to say, those who have been trained to think

critically about ideas – they sometimes acquire an unchecked momentum and an irresistible power over multitudes of men that may grow too violent to be affected by rational criticism. (Berlin, 1969, p. 1)

It is unnerving how applicable his words, shaped by the concerns of the Cold War, are to our current situation. Berlin is writing in defence of liberty and warning against the retreat in the academy from critical political engagement with difficult ideas. The problems he identifies have been magnified with demands for a non-attainable freedom from offence, further hemmed in by the fear of religious radicals or any radical voice that challenges current orthodoxies of political correctness.

Enshrining academic freedom at the heart of university life will protect wider freedoms of expression and belief. Academic freedom arises from the foundational freedom of speech. Religious freedom is deeply connected to academic freedom. The latter guarantees the liberty to question, explore, and challenge received wisdom and established orthodoxies. This is exactly what all religions have done at many points in history. The liberty that people of faith claim for themselves, especially if they are from minority faiths, is that same liberty that treasures freedom of thought and speech. To reduce faith to, at best, an emotional attachment to identity, and at worst an incitement to radical extremism means that it will by necessity occupy a negative space in the academy. Between cultural essentialism and political fear, academic freedom and the very purpose of the academy remain under threat.

Religion and the academy are not strangers to each other though they have become increasingly estranged. Faith and critical reason are similar in leading to open horizons; they both promote a belief in strong spaces of creative possibility; belief in the room for fulfilment and self- and community- realisation. Both religion and the university form the basis for an informed community. Both communities can be open or closed. They can end in dogma or enquiry. But what they stand for is essentially liberty of faith and liberty of ideas from temporal power.

Some may still argue that religious dogma is diametrically opposed to the academic tradition of engaging in rational enquiry, and the freedom to do so without external restraints. They have a right to make that argument but equally they cannot and should not use it to silence or ban faith from the academy. Ethically and practically, it would be no different to the use of religion to stifle and silence debate. Both camps need to realise that such arguments ultimately undermine their own freedom of ideas and expression.

The current danger that religion represents to academic freedom is not its tenets or its articles of faith, but its alienation from the intellectual discourse in the academy. When regulations seek to restrict and silence those who profess a faith, academic freedom is restricted and academics and scholars are silenced. When students decry their own silencing, but then adopt the mantle of victimhood and seek 'protection' from contrary views lest their faith sensibilities be hurt or challenged, they further undermine their own academic freedom.

What we are witnessing in twenty-first century Britain is a fervent zeal to enforce new socially-dictated and state-imposed orthodoxies. The new and increasingly popular doctrine of the diminished vulnerable individual coupled with a ubiquitous suspicion of liberty, are just as, if not more, harmful as religious dogma. Contemporary identity politics and security consciousness join together in seeking to vilify, ban and even criminalise certain forms of thought and speech. The new heretics are those who pose a challenge to this new dogmatism. As free-thinking academics, it behooves us to be those heretics.

It is time for the academy to rediscover its faith in its own mission and purpose, and the values of intellectual freedom and expression. It is also time for the academy to defend, promote and enforce all of the tenets of academic freedom. Encouraging a free, frank and sometimes bruising debate between advocates of faith and reason may be a good place to start.

References

Aarrevaara, T. (2010). 'Academic Freedom in a Changing Academic World' in *European Review* 18 (1).

Adams, R. (2015) 'Students' union blocks speech by "inflammatory" anti-sharia activist' in *The Guardian* (29/09/15). Available at: http://www.theguardian.com/education/2015/sep/26/student-union-blocks-speech-activist-maryam-namazie-warwick (accessed 18/01/16).

Berlin, I. (1969) 'Two Concepts of Liberty' in I. Berlin, *Four Essays on Liberty*, Oxford: Oxford University Press.

Doumani, B. (2006) 'Between Coercion and Privatization: Academic Freedom in the Twenty First Century' in B. Doumani, *Academic Freedom After September 11*. Cambridge MA: M.I.T. Press.

Durkheim, E. (1976) *The Elementary Forms of the Religious Life*. London: Allen & Unwin Ltd.

Espinoza, J. (2015) 'Lee Rigby: "E" grade Michael Adebolajo scraped into Greenwich University which was targeted by extremists' in *The Daily Telegraph* (12/03/15). Available at: http://www.telegraph.co.uk/news/uknews/terrorism-in-the-uk/11466815/Lee-Rigby-E-grade-Michael-Adebolajo-scraped-into-Greenwich-University-which-was-targeted-by-extremists.html (accessed 19/09/15).

Giroux, H. (2006) 'Academic Freedom Under Fire: The Case for Critical Pedagogy' in *College Literature* 33 (4).

Head, S. (2011) 'The Grim Threat to British Universities' in *The New York Review of Books*. Available at: http://www.nybooks.com/articles/2011/01/13/grim-threat-british-universities/ (accessed 18/01/16).

H. M. Government (2015) *Prevent Duty Guidance: for higher education institutions in England and Wales*. Available at: https://www.gov.uk/government/uploads/system/uploads/attachment_data/file/4459 16/Prevent_Duty_Guidance_For_Higher_Education__England__W ales_.pdf (accessed 18/01/16).

Ivie, R. (2005) 'A Presumption of Academic Freedom' in *Review of Education, Pedagogy and Cultural Studies* (27) pp. 53–85.

Lyons, J. (2009) *The House of Wisdom: How the Arabs Transformed Western Civilisation*. London: Bloomsbury Press.

Malik, K. (2015) 'Politics of the Disenchanted' in *Aljazeera*. (21/09/15). Available at: http://www.aljazeera.com/indepth/opinion/2015/09/politics-disenchanted-150920101229386.html (accessed 22/09/2015).

National Secular Society (2015) 'Warwick Students' Union bans ex-Muslim activist and says speakers must "avoid insulting other faiths"'. Available at: http://www.secularism.org.uk/news/2015/09/warwick-student-union-bans-ex-muslim-activist-and-says-speakers-must-avoid-insulting-other-faiths (accessed 25/09/2015).

Nelson, C. (2010) *No University is an Island: Saving Academic Freedom* New York: New York University Press.

Parfitt, T. (2015) 'Hardline Muslim students at Jihadi John's old university "refuse to speak to women"' in *The Daily Express* (21/09/15). Available at: http://www.express.co.uk/news/uk/606710/Islamic-Society-University-Westminster-Jihadi-John-report-panel-Mohammed-Emwazi-ISIS (accessed 21/09/2015).

Quinn, R. (2004) 'Defending Dangerous Minds' in *Items & Issues* (5) pp. 1–2.

Ramesh, R. and Halliday, J. (2015) 'Student accused of being a terrorist for reading book on terrorism' in *The Guardian* (24/09/15).

Russell, C. (1993) *Academic Freedom*. London: Routledge.

Sardar, Z. (2014) 'The Circumference of Freethought' in *Critical Muslim* (12) 1.

Seibold, M. (2011) 'UK: Muslim students, including trainee doctors, walking out on lectures on evolution' (28/11/11). Available at: http://www.jihadwatch.org/2011/11/uk-muslim-students-including-trainee-doctors-walking-out-on-lectures-on-evolution (accessed 19/09/15).

Slaughter, S. (1980) 'The Danger Zone: Academic Freedom and Civil Liberties' in *The Annals of the American Academy of Political and Social Science* (448) pp. 46–61.

Sullivan, W. (2005) *The Impossibility of Religious Freedom.* Princeton: Princeton University Press.

Tillich, P. (1956) *The Religious Situation.* London: Thames & Hudson.

Wuthnow, R. (2007) 'Can Faith Be More Than a Side Show in the Contemporary Academy' in D. Jacobsen and R. Jacobsen eds. *The American University in a Postsecular Age: Religion and Higher Education.* Oxford: Oxford University Press.

Yezza, H. (2008) 'Britain's terror laws have left me and my family shattered' in *The Guardian* (18/08/08). Available at: http://www.theguardian.com/commentisfree/2008/aug/18/terrorism.civilliberties (accessed 19/09/2015).

No Time for Muses: The Research Excellence Framework and the Pursuit of Mediocrity

Anthony J. Stanonis

Witnessing a growing government bureaucracy during the 1920s, American journalist H. L. Mencken unsheathed his pen. 'It is the invariable habit of bureaucracies, at all times and everywhere, to assume ... that every citizen is a criminal', he wrote in a November 1926 edition of the *Chicago Tribune*. His pen took no quarter: 'Their one apparent purpose, pursued with a relentless and furious diligence, is to convert the assumption into a fact. They hunt endlessly for proofs, and, when proofs are lacking, for suspicions' (Mencken, 1926, p. 1). Mencken's commentary recognised the tension between the liberty of citizens and the social control undertaken by government, even within a democracy. The expansion of government oversight risked bureaucratic entanglements that restricted personal freedom. If unchecked, government would turn each citizen into a modern-day 'subject' with the bureaucrat as 'lord'. Mencken was certainly prone to hyperbole, but his claims offer a worthy starting-point for evaluating the appraisal procedure known as the Research Excellence Framework (REF).

Systems for evaluating research within UK universities date to the Thatcher years, when government fully funded higher education. In 1985, Keith Joseph, the Secretary of State for Education and Science, published a green paper entitled *The Development of Higher Education into the 1990s*. The document called for a system to assess research within UK universities. Joseph eyed the vibrancy of universities within the United States. Patrick Minford, professor of applied economics at Cardiff Business School, explains, 'Indeed, the USA was the model Sir Keith had in mind that the UK, then a state monolith, should get good enough to emulate and he hoped that, once fit, would become a market-driven sector where reputation and quality would get their market rewards' (Minford, 27/07/15). He argues that rather than a temporary jolt, the evaluation process has evolved into a 'huge bureaucracy [...] devoted to corralling academics to meet the aims of the exercise' (Minford, 27/07/15). The appraisal process, born in the aftermath of the Falklands War, also reflected concerns with the decline of Britain as a global force. Not surprisingly, the REF, the most recent research appraisal process, fixates on the international reputation and supposed global impact of UK research. Research is also encouraged to address social and economic matters (Minford, 27/07/15).

The REF in 2014 consisted of four main panels responsible for overseeing the thirty-six discipline-specific subpanels. These totalled 898 academic members and 259 'research users'. The REF panels had roughly two years to assess 191,150 'research outputs' from over 52,061 full-time academic staff at 154 higher education institutions (HEFCE, 2014a and 2014b). Another 6,975 'impact case studies' were also assessed. Each submission was graded on a 4-point scale: (4) 'world-leading' (3) 'internationally excellent' (2) 'internationally recognised' (1) 'nationally recognised' (HEFCE, 2014a and 2014b: ii, 4, 7). Some items went unclassified. Impact studies were ranked similarly: (4) 'outstanding' (3) 'very considerable' (2) 'considerable' (1) 'recognised but modest' and unclassified (HEFCE, 2014a and 2014b: ii, p. 4, p. 7). These categories then provided a grade point average for institutions and their various schools.

Institutions were thereby ranked for their 'research power' calculated by multiplying a school's grade point average by the total number of its full-time faculty. Universities thus have a vested interest in pushing each faculty member to publish enough for the REF – called being 'REF returnable' – and to target projects that might receive higher grades. Academic freedom is thereby constricted as university staff scheme for better REF scores while others with low scores or too few publications – no matter how excellent or even award-winning – risk being purged, a fate already confronted by a few of my colleagues. Furthermore, an anxious, bloated university bureaucracy fixated on REF-oriented metrics has increasingly smothered the university grounded on unfettered scholarship and trust.

Despite the nomenclature and pomp, the REF panels offered shoddy coverage and expertise for the purpose at hand. In REF 2014, 30 per cent of outputs were graded a 4; 46 per cent received a 3; 20 per cent garnered a 2; 3 per cent were given a 1. Only 1 per cent went unclassified (Jump, 18/12/14). Divided per individual, this means that each panellist evaluated at least 187 articles, books, and other submissions. That amounts to 374 items if panellists worked in pairs to ensure greater fairness – as they do in double-marking significant work by students. This was all supposedly accomplished while panellists undertook their regular teaching, research and administrative demands.

For a process focused on situating UK scholarship in a global perspective, the panels paradoxically lacked evaluators from outside the UK. International participation was practically non-existent. The four main panels consisted of a foreign membership of between 10 to 25 per cent. These foreign affiliations gave a veneer of legitimacy to the REF's claims about identifying internationally important research. But the veneer crumbles upon examination of the sub-panels. None of the forty-one persons involved with Sub-Panel 30, covering the field of History, was from an institution outside the UK. Ironically, the same holds true for the thirty-nine persons who worked on Sub-Panel 28, covering the field of Modern Languages and Linguistics. Even Sub-Panel 21, assessing Politics and International Studies, contained only two members out of thirty-one who claimed affiliations outside the UK – though these two possessed joint appointments within domestic institutions. 96 per cent of UK research outputs in REF 2014 were classed as at least 'internationally recognised' (HEFCE, 2014c) meaning they covered material and were of a standard that would garner academic interest beyond the UK. Given the insularity of the sub-panels such claims are barely credible. Rather than trusting individual scholars to engage best with their specialised fields in the tradition of free and equal debate, government and universities have constructed a hollow scarecrow via the REF that, in the tradition of empire, defines international standards from the perspective of the metropole.

Criticism of the REF notes its origins in Thatcherism and the application of corporate production quotas to universities as the government has grappled with declining resources and escalating debt. Reflecting on the increased restrictions placed on academic life over the last thirty years, Terry Eagleton, a professor of English at the University of Lancaster, remarks, 'Instead of government by academics there is rule by hierarchy, a good deal of Byzantine bureaucracy, junior professors who are little but dogsbodies, and vice chancellors who behave as though they are running General Motors' (Eagleton, 06/04/15). The global prominence of American universities – especially their ability to draw international students – has stoked the envy of UK administrators struggling with budgetary cuts. UK universities have eagerly recruited foreign students because they pay higher fees. Flooding the market with publications and self-proclaiming those products as globally significant is equivalent to an American-style advertising campaign. Eagleton notes: 'What has emerged in Britain [...] is what one might call Americanization without the affluence' (Eagleton, 06/04/15).

American universities have also witnessed a dramatic growth in administrators as these institutions confront intense competition for students. However, academic freedom among American faculty has been insulated from publication quotas because of the tenure system and the dual public-private university system, which facilitates competitive hiring practices. The emphasis on student development has also given faculty greater freedom for intellectual pursuits. Wendy Brown, a political scientist at the University of California-Berkeley, elaborates:

> But only in the United States did a post-secondary education contoured toward developing the person and the citizen, not merely the job holder, come ubiquitously to structure higher education curriculums, and only in the United States was such an education on offer to a wide swath of the population from the 1940s forward. (Brown, 2011, pp. 25–26)

This emphasis on personal character and citizenship encouraged faculty to be both role models for their students as well as productive scholars. Faculty members, especially after the 1960s, were encouraged to be activists for economic equality and social justice. Brown identifies how the REF eviscerates this function of the university:

> The move to judge academic endeavor by its uptake in nonacademic venues (commerce, state agencies, NGOS), as the recently implemented British 'Research Excellent Framework' does, is equally damaging. Not only does it abjure humanistic inquiry that explores and builds meaning; it cannot capture the value of basic research from which technical applications derive, thus shutting off the spring waters whose exploitation it affirms. (Brown, 2011, p. 33)

In other words, the organic encouragement of academic research and social engagement has been ignored within the UK. The REF, like any form of Taylorism, treats researchers as cogs in a machine of mass production. Scholars' academic outputs are treated as throwaway goods with little consideration beyond the next REF.

On this point, one is reminded of David Lodge's satirical novel *Changing Places* from 1975. A well-travelled professor of English at the University of Birmingham, Lodge uses a faculty exchange programme between a US and UK university – 'Euphoric State' and 'Rummidge', respectively – to highlight the striking differences between the higher education systems and their approach to life as well as research. At Euphoric State, faculty members enjoy not only the intellectual freedom safeguarded by tenure but also a range of funding opportunities from government and private organisations. They 'picked up grants and fellowships as other men pick up hats' (1975, p. 9). Those Americans who came to Rummidge eschewed the more rigid administrative demands, convoluted marking procedures, and overall bureaucracy of the UK university system. 'Hence the American visitors to Rummidge tended to be young and/or undistinguished, determined Anglophiles who could find no other way of getting to England or, very rarely, specialists in one of the esoteric disciplines in which Rummidge, through the support of local industry, had established an unchallenged supremacy: domestic appliance technology, tyre sciences and the biochemistry of the cocoa bean' (1975, p. 9). The appraisal procedures implemented since the 1980s were meant to galvanise the research agenda at universities like the fictional Rummidge while also making UK researchers aware of global needs. Ironically, appraisal systems such as the REF have instead exacerbated the flaws within the UK's Rummidges by increasing bureaucratic structures, fixating on ill-conceived metrics, and eroding the freedom of academic staff to undertake research as each sees fit.

The REF is grounded on a good intention. Faculty should be engaged with the intellectual life of their respective fields rather than resting on their laurels.

The REF requires a faculty member to submit four research outputs – books, articles, patents, conference proceedings, performances, exhibitions, or other work – in order to be eligible for evaluation. Fewer submissions are required of faculty who undertook maternity leave or a career break during the evaluated period. Some items can be double-weighted 'if an output is of sufficient scale and scope to merit double-weighting in the assessment' (HEFCE, 2011, p. 14).

However, the REF's emphasis on outputs and speed encourages mediocrity rather than excellence. Even if a book achieved significance in scale and scope, a tome – at best – it gets double-weighted. Academics in the humanities are thus punished for writing books rather than articles. Their freedom to develop arguments is truncated, even though major international and national associations, especially within the humanities, privilege such work through prominent book awards. Worse, the REF has contributed to the publication of slipshod edited collections and new journals, mainly online, with no track record and little readership. An American reviewer of *The Oxford Handbook of Tudor Drama*, for instance, noted the curious lack of contributors from US and Canadian institutions and the odd inclusion of self-citations in lieu of more prominent scholarship. The reviewer blamed 'England's unforgiving Research Excellence Framework' (Hornback, 2013, p. 746). He wrote, 'As ever more rigid assessment regimes worldwide exert greater pressures to publish, to be cited, and to cite colleagues (but not to include or cite others), this collection points to the need for resisting such demands' (Hornback, 2013, p. 746). In other words, rapid production and dissemination of scholarship under the REF undermines rather than bolsters the international reputation of UK universities.

An anthropological analysis by Cris Shore and Susan Wright has exposed how scholars and university administrators purposely undermined or manipulated their work in order to satisfy the REF requirements. Efforts to scheme the REF highlight ways academic freedom and integrity have been sacrificed. They argue:

> The skewing effects of systems of measuring and grading universities' research output are now so familiar that they have acquired their own terminology, such as 'salami slicing' (cutting research results into small chunks, each published as a separate journal article), 'rushing to press' (publishing partial results as soon as they are available rather than making a mature and considered analysis), and the 'star player' syndrome (hiring high-profile researchers just before a research assessment exercise. (Shore and Wright, 2015, p. 425, p. 430)

The result is a profound 'deprofessionalisation' within universities.

The emphasis on quantity undermines quality – the hallmark of academic freedom – in numerous ways. The need to publish and to do so in impressive journals has a counterproductive impact. Michael Bailey argues that targeting '"top" journals forces academics to fashion their research around what those journals want, which can result in an unwillingness to push beyond the narrow confines of specialist fields of study and, ultimately, intellectual inertia' (Bailey, 2011, p. 96).

He rightly highlights the corrosive effect of the REF on university life. Bailey writes that:

> With sails trimmed tight, increasingly academics are forced to cut corners if they are to meet the next publishing deadline, particularly newly qualified academics who are expected to combine research with heavy teaching loads and endless duties (a problem whose sheer scale and mind-numbingly tedious and pointless nature appears to be exclusively British). (Bailey, 2011, p. 96)

The requirement that each faculty member submit four publications further undermines intellectual activity in numerous ways. Within the humanities, for example, this one-size-fits-all approach to assessing academic production ignores disciplinary, geographical, and temporal specialisations. A historian working on Africa or the United States must submit the same number of publications as a historian of the United Kingdom. No consideration is given for the distance required to reach and undertake a prolonged stay at the archival holdings. A literary scholar analysing easily accessible novels submits the same number of publications as an anthropologist, despite the potentially time-consuming fieldwork required for the latter. The REF thereby handicaps much of the internationally important research it seeks to inspire by forcing conformity upon academics.

Individual publication targets are detrimental to creativity and fail to engage with the unique trajectory of each academic project, in which time is the most precious commodity. A perusal of the acknowledgements within academic books reveals the extraordinary number of years invested in these volumes. As already mentioned, the REF discourages such sophisticated scholarly analysis by fixating upon the number of publications. Instead of individual targets, reasonable departmental targets might work better by providing a stronger sense of community within a discipline-specific school. But even departmental targets risk starting a school down a steep slippery slope. A school, for instance, that reaches a 25 per cent target for REF-returnable faculty will soon face pressure to meet a more ambitious target, especially as administrators play musical chairs across the university system and therefore seek a résumé that better assures future employment.

A significant, though often overlooked, problem with the REF rests in the disproportionate representation given to higher-ranking faculty members. This imbalance particularly threatens academic freedom by reinforcing disciplinary boundaries and entrenching lines of thought. Professors dominated the review panels on the 2014 REF. Professors formed 65 per cent of Sub-Panel 21 on Politics and International Relations, 82 per cent of Sub-Panel 28 on Modern Languages and Linguistics, and 70 per cent of Sub-Panel 30 on History. Junior faculty amounted to 10 per cent of Sub-Panel 21, 0 per cent on Sub-Panel 28, and 20 per cent of Sub-Panel 30. The other members on those panels – 25 per cent, 18 per cent, and 10 per cent, respectively – were employees of the British Library, Oxford University Press, BBC, or other agencies that partner with UK universities (Jump, 18/12/14). This latter group predominantly lacked doctorates. The use of professors resides in the assumption that they are better suited to assess the quality of work because of their greater expertise – an expertise cultivated through years within the profession.

Such reliance on senior members of academia carries a profound cost. Older may mean wiser but it does not generally mean greater openness to new ideas. As Thomas Kuhn has argued in his classic *The Structure of Scientific Revolutions*, academics forge their careers by promoting their research and defending their claims from challengers. Though focused on the sciences, Kuhn's framework outlining how new knowledge gains credibility carries weight across the disciplines. A discipline works on particular problems, yet some of these problems may prove unsolvable without a completely new worldview. Einstein's theory of relativity revolutionised physics, a process unpacked by Kuhn. Yet a similar shift occurred within the field of history during the 1960s. Historians in the United States, for example, jettisoned white supremacist paradigms, such as that of the so-called Dunning School, for one inclusive of African American and minority perspectives. As a result, once marginalised scholars, such as W. E. B. Du Bois, gained widespread recognition for being ahead of their time. Since the 1990s, younger scholars have pioneered the now-established fields of tourism studies, queer studies, and food studies. Kuhn explains that innovators tend to be 'so young or so new to the crisis-ridden field that practice has committed them less deeply than most of their contemporaries to the world view and rules determined by the old paradigm' (Kuhn, 1970, p. 144). Innovation typically occurs despite rather than because of older intellectuals. Kuhn concedes that 'most of them can be reached in one way or another' (Kuhn, 1970, p. 152). However, some intellectuals, 'particularly the older and more experienced ones, may resist indefinitely' the work of younger scholars (Kuhn, 1970, p. 152).

The depth of modern knowledge and the development of the university system have increased the age of innovators during the twentieth century. Whereas scholars typically became research active by 23 in 1900, they did not become research active until 31 in 2000 (Jones, 2010, pp. 1–2). Drawing from the fields of Chemistry, Medicine, Physics, and Economics, Benjamin Jones, a professor at the Kellogg School of Management at Northwestern University, has shown that the 'mean age at great achievement for both Nobel Prize winners and great technological inventors rose by about six years over the course of the twentieth century' (Jones, 2010, pp. 1–2). Yet he found 'no compensating shift in the productivity of innovators beyond middle age' (Jones, 2010, pp. 1–2). In other words, notable innovations are most likely to occur between the ages of 30 and 40, peaking around 38 then decreasing in likelihood later in life. I would contend that a similar curve occurs within the humanities.

The wisdom and experience of professors should not be discarded but, rather, there needs to be balance to ensure more accurate ranking and greater openness to cutting-edge scholarship. Privileging professors over junior faculty dulls the intellectual environment by causing a chilling effect on academic freedom, especially when livelihoods are at risk due to the REF. Unpopular topics or adventurous projects are implicitly discouraged. This is precisely the situation condemned by Jürgen Habermas when he called for the 'democratisation of the university' during the late 1960s. Habermas proposed, 'The university run by professors, which simulates a community of teachers and students, would be replaced by a corporation in whose administration all three parties would take part with the opportunity of asserting their own interests: students, junior faculty, and professors' (Habermas, 1971, pp. 11–2). The REF falls far short of this ideal and the safeguards this ideal provides for academic freedom, intellectual vibrancy, and open community across the generations. Writing for the *Guardian* in 2014, Derek Sayer, professor of history at Lancaster University, warned:

> The most innovative work – the research that breaks molds, shifts paradigms and redefines fields – may not even make it into the REF at all because universities tailor their submission to what they think REF panels want, and REF panels reflect disciplinary hierarchies. (Sayer, 15/12/14)

Echoing Habermas a half century ago, he further stressed that the 'REF panels give extraordinary gatekeeping power to a disproportionately older, male, white – and overwhelmingly Russell Group and former 1994 Group – academic elite' (Sayer, 15/12/14).

Rather than containing the damage caused by the REF, the bureaucracies of universities and of government increasingly reshape higher education policies to bolster the REF rankings. Growing pressure to attain grants, which the UK universities siphon, is further curtailing academic freedom in the name of fostering outputs. This curtailment is also reflected on the recently introduced requirement to publish in open-access journals, as demanded for grants funded by the UK government and for the inclusion of articles in the next REF. The fixation with the REF reaches beyond faculty to postgraduates. Students studying for their doctorates are increasingly under pressure to work along models forced upon faculty. This undermines their standing on the global job market and constrains their intellectual ingenuity. Like a virus, the REF has penetrated deep into the UK university system, consuming the very host that gives it life.

Studies have shown that innovation in academia requires an intellectual culture that provides faculty ample time to pursue their ideas. Innovation also demands an acceptance that some adventurous projects fail. Both aspects require trust in the wisdom and devotion of scholars – a trust the REF denies by its very nature. The American universities' tenure system allows for both time and failure; the REF truncates the time available for research and punishes failure to such a degree that faculty are discouraged from pursuing radical new concepts, experiments, or innovations. The REF is converting universities into research treadmills by pushing faculty to great exertions in terms of outputs but encouraging them to go nowhere in terms of ideas. As Mencken warned: 'Long before the bureaucracy is satisfied, the man is worn out and in despair' (14/11/26).

References

Bailey, M. (2011) 'The Academic as Truth-Teller' in M. Bailey and D. Freedman, eds., *The Assault on Universities: A Manifesto for Resistance.* London: Pluto Press.

Brown, W. (2011) 'The End of Educated Democracy' in *Representations* (116) 1, pp. 19–41.

Donoghue, F. (2008) *The Last Professors: The Corporate University and the Fate of the Humanities.* New York: Fordham University Press.

Eagleton, T. (2015) 'The Slow Death of the University' in *The Chronicle of Higher Education* (06/04/15).

Ginsberg, B. (2011) *The Fall of the Faculty: The Rise of the All-Administrative University and Why It Matters.* New York: Oxford University Press.

Tuchman, G. (2009) *Wannabe U: Inside the Corporate University.* Chicago: University of Chicago Press.

Habemas, J. (1971) *Toward a Rational Society: Student Protest, Science, and Politics.* London: Heinemann Educational Books.

Higher Education Funding Council for England. (2011) *Assessment Framework and Guidance on Submissions.* Available at: http:// www.ref.ac.uk/media/ref/content/pub/assessmentframeworkand guidanceonsubmissions/GOS%20including%20addendum.pdf (accessed on 11/09/15).

Higher Education Funding Council for England. (2014) *Research Excellence Framework 2014: The Results.* Available at: http://www. ref.ac.uk/media/ref/content/pub/REF%2001%202014%20-%20 introduction.pdf (accessed 20/08/15).

Hornback, R. (2013) 'Review of the Oxford Handbook of Tudor Drama' in *Renaissance Quarterly* (66) 2.

Jones, B. (2010) 'Age and Great Invention' in *The Review of Economics and Statistics* (92), pp. 1–14.

Jump, P. (2014) 'REF 2014: Results by subject' in *Times Higher Education* (18/12/14). Available at: https://www.timeshighereducation. co.uk/features/ref-2014-results-by-subject/2017594.article (accessed 20/08/15).

Kuhn, T. (1970) *The Structure of Scientific Revolutions* Chicago: University of Chicago Press, 2nd Ed.

Lodge, D. (1993) 'Changing Places,' in *A David Lodge Trilogy* London: Penguin.

Mencken, H. L. (1926) 'Life Under Bureaucracy' in *Chicago Tribune* (14/11/26).

Minford, P. (2015) 'Why the Government Should Abolish the Research Excellence Framework' in *Institute of Economic Affairs blog* (27/07/15). Available at: http://www.iea.org.uk/blog/why-the-government-should-abolish-the-research-excellence-framework#.Vb YLdPF2duc (accessed 12/09/15).

REF 2014 (2014). *Panel Membership.* Available at: http://www. ref.ac.uk/panels/panelmembership/ (accessed 23/08/15).

Sayer, D. (2014) 'Five reasons why the REF is not fit for purpose' in *The Guardian* (15/12/14). Available at: http://www.theguardian.com/ higher-education-network/2014/dec/15/research-excellence-framework-five-reasons-not-fit-for-purpose (accessed 20/08/15).

Shore, C. and Wright, S. (2015) 'Audit Culture Revisited: Rankings, Ratings, and the Reassembling of Society' in *Current Anthropology* (56) 3. pp. 421–444.

Twitchell, J. (2004) *Branded Nation: The Marketing of Megachurch, College Inc., and Museumworld.* New York: Simon and Schuster.

Part Three

Threats to Academic Freedom

Academic Freedom in an Age of Terror?

Tara McCormack

The current Counter-Terrorism and Security Act places legal responsibility, known as the Prevent Duty, on universities to demonstrate that they are actively countering radicalisation and preventing terrorism. Quite what this really means is still open to question, however it will have and is having a chilling effect on academic freedom, in particular on free speech, discussion and teaching within universities.

Freedom of speech within the university is the foundation of academic freedom more broadly. The university occupies a special position in a liberal democratic society and that is to be a place in which people should be entirely at liberty to argue, explore and contest *all* ideas, especially those that are hateful, unpleasant and/or controversial. This is not for the glory of the individual institutions but for the greater good of society. In the words of the 1940 Declaration of the American Association of University Professors (AAUP); the common good depends upon the free search for truth and its free exposition.

Despite having a chilling effect on academic freedom, the Prevent Duty will not resolve any security problems. The attractions of Jihadism have very little to do with radicalisation as commonly understood. The chapter is structured as follows: in this first section I look at what the Prevent Duty is and what the government expects it to achieve. In the second section I look at some of the obvious problems that this policy entails and the immediate consequences in terms of freedom of speech and discussion in the university. In the third section I argue that the Prevent Duty represents a fundamentally bad faith exercise in that the attractions of Jihad are to be found in the domestic realm. Pragmatically, this legislation makes institutions responsible for something that is outside of their control and will result in a vast bureaucratic structure used by institutions to cover their own backs. These measures will simply erode liberal democratic freedoms further and strengthen the attractions of Jihad.

The Prevent Duty

On 21st September 2015 the government's Prevent Duty became a legal obligation for British universities. This new legal duty has come into force as part of the government's Counter-Terrorism and Security Act 2015 (CTSA). This means that British universities now have a legal duty in their day to day functioning to 'have due regard to the need to prevent people from being drawn into terrorism' (H. M. Government, 2015a, p. 3). The Prevent Duty that is part of the CTSA is not just focused on universities but applies to all public institutions in England and Wales. For example, in July 2015 all schools and child care providers (meaning also nurseries and child minders) also became legally obliged to comply with the Prevent Duty (Department for Education, 2015).

The Prevent Duty derives from the government's Contest anti-terrorism strategy, which consists of four parts; Pursue, Protect, Prevent, Prepare (Home Office, 2015). The Prevent part of the anti-terrorism strategy is designed to stop people becoming terrorists or supporting terrorism and extremism (Home Office, 2015). The aim of the Prevent Duty for universities introduced in the CTSA bill is ostensibly clear. It is to stop extremists radicalising students on university campuses; to tackle gender segregation at events and to support students at risk of radicalisation (Prime Minister's Office, 2015). It is also part of the government's strategy to build a more cohesive society.

The government has issued guidance for higher education institutions as to how they can demonstrate compliance with the Prevent Duty. Firstly, the focus is on speakers and events. For example, when inviting external speakers, universities must make sure that they are complying with the numerous legal duties and obligations in terms of restrictions on speech already in place. For example, inciting hatred against a person on the grounds of their race or religion or sexual orientation or vocally supporting a proscribed terrorist group are already criminal acts.

There are also a number of other laws (to do with equalities legislation) that criminalise harassment or discrimination based on gender or religion that are part of the Prevent Duty framework. So for example, institutions must pay particular regard to issues of gender segregation at university events. This is because some university Islamic societies have been holding events with gender segregated seating. There is also legislation about safety and welfare that universities have a duty to follow (Universities UK, 2013).

Universities are also expected to keep a close eye on their students as students who have been radicalised off campus are understood to be a problem. Changes in a student's behaviour, for example, are to be noted. The Contest counter-terrorism strategy was developed under the Labour government in 2003.

Thus when we discuss Prevent we are discussing a number of already existing measures and legal obligations that are about preventing people being drawn into terrorism. The Prevent Duty has not in itself created new legal obligations and duties as such. What the Prevent Duty *does* do is give universities explicit orders that they must actively demonstrate how they are fulfilling all these existing legal obligations and duties. Therefore, universities must be able to *demonstrate* that they have mechanisms in place to make proper actions plans, risk assessments, IT policies and staff training to ensure compliance (H. M. Government, 2015b). All of this applies to the main body of the university but also to students' unions (which are in law separate bodies but subject to many of the same legal obligations), and other organisations or institutions that are part of the universities.

While this chapter will be discussing current developments under the Conservative government, it needs to be kept in mind that Prevent itself and the ideas and assumptions that underlie it are part of a cross party consensus on the causes of so-called radicalisation and how to deal with it. The current CTSA itself is part of a number of on-going measures, including a new five-year plan to deal with extremism and a Counter Extremism Bill that will be forthcoming later this year (Dearden, 2015). Cameron has stated that the government's anti-extremism strategy will also entail actively building a more cohesive society (Greirson, 2015).

Curtailing academic freedom in the name of preventing radicalisation

There are many obvious problems with the current sprawling legal regime. The numerous obligations on universities mean that academic freedom within universities is curtailed. In particular, freedom of speech within universities is limited. Without freedom of speech in the university, there is no academic freedom. However, curtailing freedom of speech within the university is explicitly the point of the numerous prohibitions. The argument made is straightforward and open. Freedom of speech is allowed only up to a certain point within any British university. Freedom of political and religious speech is allowed to the point that it does not contravene the laws on say, incitement to hatred based on religion, or sex. A religious speaker who for example argues that homosexuality is a punishable perversion would be committing a criminal act as that would be categorised as inciting hatred on the basis of sexuality. Thus academic freedom is severely curtailed today within British universities. There have been many examples in the last few years of universities and students' unions dis-inviting or banning speakers because they will fall foul of legal obligations.

Even under previous counter-terrorism legislation universities were considered problematic sites of radicalisation and extremism because they were thought to be places in which it was easy for radical ideas to spread. It is of course the case that over the last decade or so a small number of high-profile university educated British Muslims have engaged in murder in the name of Islam. For example, one of the murderers of Daniel Pearl was privately educated Ahmed Omar Saeed Sheikh, who attended the London School of Economics for one year. However, the Prevent Duty under the CSTA focuses even more on British universities as problematic sites of radicalisation and extremism. As part of the launch of the Prevent Duty, Cameron 'named and shamed' a number of British universities that that had hosted extremist speakers (Whitehead, 2015).

With friends like these...

There have been a number of sensible critiques made from within the university establishment of the Prevent Duty. In particular, attention has been drawn to the fact that the Prevent Duty will have an adverse effect on academic freedom. Sally Hunt, the leader of the academic trade union, the University and College Union (UCU), has strongly argued that the Prevent Duty will mean that universities will shy away from difficult subjects that could end up falling foul of the laws on, for example, incitement. The university, argues Hunt, must be a forum in which difficult subjects can be discussed (Hunt, 2015). The National Union of Students (NUS) has also made official objections to the Prevent Duty on the basis of academic freedom (Whittaker, 2015). This is all absolutely right. Of all institutions in society, universities must be a genuinely safe space in which students can argue, debate, be upset and be exposed to difficult and unpleasant ideas and opinions. Without this, the university is no longer a university.

However, a fundamental problem here is that UCU and NUS have systematically eroded academic freedom when it comes to difficult subjects. Both institutions have supported the 'no platforming' of everyone from feminist Julie Bindel to anti-Sharia campaigner Maryam Namazie. So it is rather surprising to hear the case for academic freedom being made here. If one refuses to accept Julie Bindel the renowned British feminist because of her (most would say non-controversial and non-hateful) views on transgender people, then it is highly unlikely that the National Union of Students will come out in support of a radical Islamic preacher who thinks homosexuals should be stoned to death. In order for the NUS or UCU to fight for freedom of speech both need to argue against the idea of 'no platform' as whole.

A second argument that has been made from within the university is that Prevent is a fundamentally racist duty that will criminalise Muslim and Black students by making them objects of suspicion and surveillance. There is good evidence of this, demonstrated by a recent preposterous example. Staffordshire University postgraduate student Umar, who is studying for a master's degree in Terrorism, Crime and Global Security, was found reading a book called *Terrorism Studies* in his university library. He was hauled off for questioning by university security. Unfortunately, this is not a new problem. In 2008 Hicham Yezza was arrested and prosecuted at the University of Nottingham for research related activities (Yezza, 2015). Certainly Prevent as a whole has been argued to increase fear and alienation of Muslim communities in the UK and there is little reason to doubt this (Anderson, 2015) as even children are being reported (Whitehead, 2015b).

However, within universities there also exists a counter-veiling fear of being branded racist. So for example, university administrations are knowingly allowing gender segregation at Islamic Society events. Regardless of whether one agrees that university societies should be allowed to make their own decisions or not, the fact of the matter is that university societies are governed by equalities laws and thus gender segregated society meetings are against the law. One can only imagine the reaction if the rugby society hosted an all-male event or if the UKIP society hosted a 'UK-born only' event. There is merit to the argument that the Prevent Duty criminalises and will criminalise Muslim students but it co-exists with university administrations allowing Islamic societies freedoms that would not be allowed to other student groups.

An exercise in bad faith

Current criticisms of Prevent have much merit to them. But whilst there are racist and problematic aspects to Prevent, the government argues that such legislation is necessary in order to prevent radicalisation, terrorism and ultimately to build a more cohesive society. It is the traditional argument that liberty and security must be balanced. Of course there *is* an argument to be made that limiting freedom is necessary in order to create a safe, secure and cohesive society.

However, the point of this chapter is to consider the specific case for Prevent and academic freedom. My argument here is that even if one accepted these restrictions on academic freedom in the cause of preventing radicalisation, extremism, terrorism and building a more cohesive society, that is, that the university must be sacrificed in order to save society, the Prevent Duty cannot achieve any of this. This is because radicalisation is very little to do with radical preachers as such or exposure to bad foreign ideas. Rather these measures will simply further erode the case for liberal democratic values and society and increase the attractions of radical Islam for a minority of British young people.

The fundamental problem with the government's Prevent Duty is that it is an exercise in bad faith. It is certainly true that a number of young British people feel so angry and or alienated from their own society that they seek to commit murder in their own country (and have successfully done so) or travel abroad to join Jihadi groups. The current social context is of course the growing number of young British (and European) Muslim men and women who have travelled to join ISIS.

The problem with the assumptions of the government (and of previous governments) that underlie these policies is that they are based upon a fundamentally flawed idea of why young people join up with ISIS or seek out radical preachers. For the government, the narrative is simple. There is a thing called 'radicalisation' and it entails young people being seduced or beguiled or simply brain-washed by radical preachers or ISIS publicity on the internet. This straightforward process makes young British people espouse radical Islamist ideas and reject mainstream Western ideas about sexual equality, secularism and so on. Or, in the worst case scenario, radicalisation motivates them to travel to Syria or Iraq and join the Jihad.

In this respect, radicalisation is a simple problem. In the same way that young people should be protected from sex offenders, young people should be protected from poisonous radical religious ideas that will turn their heads and send them off to commit atrocities in the name of some skewed vision of Islam. Cameron specifically uses the term 'grooming' (Dearden, 2015). Thus the obvious answer is to stop exposure to these radical ideas and protect vulnerable young people from wicked preachers who promote these ideas.

This has been the main assumption behind the Prevent Duty since it was launched in 2003. The London bombings in 2005 in which four young British men blew themselves up on the London Underground, killing themselves and murdering 52 people, simply served to entrench this narrative. A narrative that runs alongside is that a lack of opportunity will push young people away from mainstream society and increase the attractions of radical Islamist ideas (hence Cameron's cohesive society ideas). The problem is, this narrative bears little relationship to real life.

There *is* clearly a serious problem of alienation felt by those seeking out radical Islamic, anti-Western views or travelling to Syria to join the Jihad. However, this is a result of a much more complex process that is not to do with being brainwashed by radical preachers nor being pushed out by a hostile British (or other European) society. The journey from average Western teen/young person to radical rejection of liberal democratic society (or in worst case scenario committing mass murder at home or abroad) is a far less obvious and far more complex process than the government narrative allows. Government assumptions start at the end point of the Western Jihadis view and assume that this explains the journey (Malik, 2015).

First of all, the relationship between radical ideas and young people who adopt them is the opposite to brainwashing. Young people seek out these ideas and arguments; they are 'self-radicalised' rather than seduced into a world of evil. The London Underground bombers are a good example of this. Thus the radical preachers and ISIS videos are sought out by those already feeling alienated. The starting point is a rejection of liberal democratic society and values and a desire to search for alternative moral and religious frameworks through which to give meaning to life (see for example, Sageman, 2008).

Thus although it may seem impossible for most people of all faiths and of none to understand, there is often a great deal of romantic idealism attached to an individual's choice to join ISIS, for example. Notable work has been done on this by Dr Katherine Brown of King's College London. Brown's in-depth research has focused on British women choosing to join or support ISIS. Amongst other things, Brown has found that joining the Jihad is seen as positive step towards building a good and better society. In this respect going to Syria is an act of positive idealism (Brown, 2014).

Arguments about lack of opportunity and deprivation driving young Muslims into acts of violence are not borne out either (Sageman, 2008). This is not to claim that British society is free from racial and or class barriers, far from it. But the levels of education or professional employment of British Muslims as a whole certainly does not suggest a society in which to be born a Muslim condemns one to a life of poverty and deprivation (Gani, 2015). Moreover, British Muslims of a generation or two earlier experienced a far more racist society without turning to radical Islamist ideas.

Now the idea that young Western Muslims join the Jihad rather than set off on a gap year to poorer areas of the world cannot be understood outside of very complex set of specific circumstances and broader social factors such as the development of official multiculturalism. Such arguments lie outside of the parameters of this short chapter. The point here is that it is clear that the government's simple narrative of brainwashing and/or social rejection does not hold up when the problem is investigated seriously (Malik, 2015).

The question that is obvious from any of the serious analysis and research on the topic is why is there such a sense of rejection of their own society amongst a small minority of British people and a perception that going to join the Jihad presents a fulfilling vision of life. Why do young British people seek out Islamist ideas? This of course is a complex question to which there are no straightforward 'child protection' type solutions. It is notable that the government is aware on some level that there is a much more complex dimension to 'radicalisation' than exposure to radical Islamist ideas, hence current pledges to build a more cohesive society.

However, the solutions proposed by the government are themselves fairly empty. Cameron pledges to bring our communities together and give opportunities for all; promoting British values; giving a platform to more 'moderate' Muslims. These are great sound bites but what do they mean in practice? What does it mean to promote British values? Promoting liberty and freedom that the government is undermining with its expanding restrictions on free speech? State sponsorship of 'on-message' Muslim speakers ignores the well-known reality that young British Muslims who seek to join ISIS have already actively rejected mainstream Islam. Moreover, given that British multicultural policy of the last few decades has explicitly been premised on state patronage of specific religious or ethnic identities, the government is caught in a contradiction.

Cameron's vague grasp that the problem is much more complex than one of 'grooming' explains also why the Prevent Duty is simply restating what are already criminal acts. It is notable that the Prevent Duty fits into a broader pattern of what has been dubbed by critics 'legislative hyperactivity' that began under New Labour. The problem is not just a relentless churning out of legislation but new legislation that simply repeats things that are already illegal acts. At best this is legislation as displacement activity, being seen to be doing something. At worst it simply contributes to eroding freedom of speech and of religion, in the very places they should be protected.

Another impact of the Prevent Duty under the new legislation is that it is making universities very nervous and leading to a general clamping down on political speech. As is customary with these kinds of measures, it is being used to police other political activities. Prevent has targeted everything from campaigns against pay cuts to anti-Israeli protests. Thus this Duty will further curtail general political freedom in the university.

It is impossible, in reality, to prove or disprove where a person might have been 'radicalised' and therefore there is an increasing nervousness among university managers and administrators of being found guilty of *not* complying with the Prevent Duty. This will inevitably lead to a rise in such ridiculous cases as the Staffordshire University student discussed above in which nervous university administrations act on the basis of better safe than sorry. This will of course have the obvious effect of creating an increasingly hostile atmosphere at universities in which Muslim students are objects of suspicion who will be having to constantly 'prove' their innocence or be at risk of being hauled off for questioning. This is unlikely to decrease any sense of alienation from mainstream society.

The immediate practical outcome of the Prevent Duty, one that is already clunking into place with the recruitment of Prevent officers, is the establishment of a large bureaucratic structure that will be put in place in order to demonstrate compliance with the Prevent Duty. This will be along the lines of the equal opportunities structures in place in universities, consisting of committees, risk registers, training courses and various other structures. Thus there will be a vast structure that will spring up to demonstrate compliance.

The answer is free speech and more free speech

The problem for the government is that banning radical speakers from university campuses will do nothing to promote a cohesive society or stop young people from becoming radicalised. The clamp down on free speech in universities undermines the case for an enlightened liberal society to which the government wants to draw disenfranchised youth. Banning radical Islamic preachers will simply add grist to the mill of those disaffected and make claims to liberal freedoms ring hollow and hypocritical, which under the current anti-free speech regime they are.

The university does have a specific duty to be a truly safe space for ideas, a place in which no ideas or speakers are censored. Universities have a specific role here to promote and allow *all* types of free speech. Not just radical Islamic preachers but those arguing against

Islam, those arguing for and against anything. The university should be exactly the place where all students can make their arguments and explore their opinions. If students want to argue in favour of ISIS and invite speakers in support of ISIS, then universities need to let it happen. Of course they also need to allow speakers who are critical of ISIS and of Islam in general to speak. This would be to allow the promise of a free liberal democratic society to become true. Free speech is a fundamental freedom necessary to human flourishing and ultimately to creating a better society. However, in order for this to even begin to be realised, there would have to be a dismantling of the existing restrictions on speech. As has been argued above, the Prevent Duty is part of a growing network of restrictions on free speech and cannot be countered on its own.

References

Anderson, D. (2015) *Terrorism Acts in 2014 Report*. Available at: https://terrorismlegislationreviewer.independent.gov.uk/wp-content/uploads/2015/09/Terrorism-Acts-Report-2015_web-version.pdf (accessed 18/01/16).

Brown, K. (2014) 'Analysis: Why are Western women joining Islamic State?' (06/10/14) BBC website. Available at: http://www.bbc.co.uk/news/uk-29507410 (accessed 18 /01/16).

Dearden, L. (2015) 'David Cameron extremism speech' in *The Independent*, (20/06/15). Available at: http://www.independent.co.uk/news/uk/politics/david-cameron-extremism-speech-read-the-transcript-in-full-10401948.html (accessed 18/01/16).

Department for Education. (2015) *The Prevent Duty* (01/06/15). Available at: https://www.gov.uk/government/uploads/system/uploads/attachment_data/file/439598/prevent-duty-departmental-advice-v6.pdf (accessed 18/01/16).

Gani, A. (2015) 'Muslim population in England and Wales nearly doubles in 10 years' in *The Guardian* (11/02/15). Available at: http://www.theguardian.com/world/2015/feb/11/muslim-population-england-wales-nearly-doubles-10-years (accessed 18 /01/16).

Grierson, J. (2015) 'The four pillars of David Cameron's counter-extremism strategy' in *The Guardian* (20/07/15). Available at: http://www.theguardian.com/politics/2015/jul/20/the-four-pillars-of-david-camerons-counter-extremism-strategy (accessed 18 /01/16).

H. M. Government (2015a) *Prevent Duty Guidance*. Available at: http://www.legislation.gov.uk/ukdsi/2015/9780111133309/pdfs/u kdsiod_9780111133309_en.pdf (accessed 31/03/16).

H. M. Government. (2015b) *Prevent Duty Guidance for higher education institutions in England and Wales*. Available at: https://www.gov.uk/government/uploads/system/uploads/attachment_data/file/445916/Prevent_Duty_Guidance_For_Higher_Education __England__Wales_.pdf (accessed 18 /01/16).

Home Office. (2015) *CONTEST Annual Report 2014*. Available at: https://www.gov.uk/government/publications/contest-uk-strategy-for-countering-terrorism-annual-report-for-2014 (accessed 18 /01/16).

Hunt, S. (2015) 'Universities must not shy away from difficult subjects' in *The Daily Telegraph*, (18/09/15). Available at: http://www.telegraph.co.uk/education/educationopinion/118738 64/Universities-must-not-shy-away-from-difficult-subjects.html. (Accessed 18 /01/16).

Malik, K. (2015) 'Beyond the clichés about radicalisation' in *Pandaemonium* (22/07/15). Available at: https://kenanmalik. wordpress.com/2015/07/22/beyond-the-cliches-about-radicalisation/ (accessed 18 /01/16).

Prime Minister's Office. (2015) *PM's Extremism Taskforce: tackling extremism in universities and colleges*. Available at: https:// www.gov.uk/government/news/pms-extremism-taskforce-tackling-extremism-in-universities-and-colleges-top-of-the-agenda (accessed 18 /01/16).

Sageman, M. (2008) *Leaderless Jihad: Terror Networks in the Twenty-First Century*. Philadelphia: University of Pennsylvania Press.

Universities UK. (2013) 'External speakers in higher education institutions' (22/11/13). Available at: http://www.universitiesuk.ac.uk/ highereducation/Pages/Externalspeakersinhighereducationinstituti ons.aspx#.VowWxEulmFJ (accessed 18 /01/16).

Whitehead, T. (2015) 'British universities that give the floor to extremists are named and shamed' in *The Daily Telegraph* (17/09/15). Available at: http://www.telegraph.co.uk/education/universityeducation/11870429/British-universities-that-give-the-floor-to-extremist-speakers-are-named-and-shamed.html (accessed 18 /01/16).

Whitehead, T. (2015b) 'Children at risk of radicalisation to double' in *The Daily Telegraph* (27/07/15). Available at: http://www.telegraph.co.uk/news/uknews/terrorism-in-the-uk/11765877/Children-at-risk-of-radicalisation-to-double.html (accessed 18 /01/16).

Whittaker, F. (2015) 'NUS rejects call to back government's counter-terrorism prevent duty for colleges' in *FE Week*, (17/09/15). Available at: http://feweek.co.uk/2015/09/17/nus-rejects-calls-to-back-governments-counter-terrorism-prevent-duty-for-colleges/ (accessed 18 /01/16).

Yezza, H. (2015) 'Prevent will discourage the very students who can help fight extremism' in *The Guardian* (28/09/15). Available at: http://www.theguardian.com/commentisfree/2015/sep/28/prevent-discourage-muslim-fight-extremism-counter-terrorism-university-school-students-suspicion (accessed 18/01/16).

Changing the Subject: The Rise of 'Vulnerable' Students

Kathryn Ecclestone

Universities in the UK and in America are experiencing a rapid increase in student-led demands for 'trigger warnings' for course materials and lecture content that might generate offence on racist, sexist or homophobic grounds, memories of traumatic events, or feelings of distress. These accompany growing demands for bans on particular topics or speakers in external events (see Hume, 2015). Concerns about students' psychological and emotional vulnerability come also from staff in support and counselling services and pastoral tutoring roles who report an increase in the numbers of students presenting themselves as in need of emotional support for a widening range of problems. Challenge or resistance to these trends is increasingly presented as 'microaggression', namely acts of oppression or discrimination. The cumulative effect is to privilege claims that students are, in different ways, too vulnerable to engage with difficult or contentious materials and ideas, over the crucial role of universities in promoting academic freedom.

These phenomena and wider erosions of academic freedom cannot be understood without reference to the intertwining of vulnerability, harm, risk and resilience as 'a cultural metaphor, a resource drawn upon by a range of parties to characterise individuals and groups and to describe an increasingly diverse array of human experience' (Frawley, 2014, p. 11). Other scholars have characterised this cultural dimension as a 'vulnerability zeitgeist' (Brown, 2015) or 'an age of vulnerability' (Furedi, 2004; see also McLaughlin, 2012). However, as I shall argue, the relationship between vulnerability as a cultural metaphor and academic freedom is also inextricably bound up with long-running criticism of the oppressive effects of traditional curriculum subjects at all levels of the education system.

To explore these relationships, I first outline how the current creep of vulnerability in official policy and everyday institutional systems and practices is, in part, driven by influential arguments that vulnerability should be harnessed as the latest 'progressive' turn in older educational debates about social justice. I then argue that, far from being progressive, concerns couched in terms of care, inclusion and social justice contribute to two types of threats to academic freedom: first, overtly, through bans, trigger warnings and other calls to constrain educational practices; and, second, much more subtly and pervasively, through the increasing framing of vulnerability through cautious, self-censoring interactions with students and colleagues. The first type is at least obvious and therefore amenable to debate about its implications while the second, already endemic in schools, seems slowly to be becoming an accepted, routine part of everyday academic life and is therefore much less visible. I use proposals in the government's Prevent Duty for universities to detect and report 'vulnerability to radicalisation' (UK Government 2015) to highlight some stark consequences of the educational climate created by both these manifestations of vulnerability. I conclude by suggesting some resistances and challenges to these developments.

The creep of vulnerability

There has been a very significant expansion of official criteria for defining 'the vulnerable' as targets for diverse forms of state intervention across social and welfare policy between 1998 and 2010 (see Brown, 2015 and McLaughlin, 2012). This expansion has continued under the previous coalition and current Conservative governments. In schools, for example, the Office for Standards in Education defines migrant children, those with special educational needs, pupils who are disengaged or who are simply not meeting their targets and therefore need 'additional support' as vulnerable (OFSTED, 2012). Here vulnerability widens almost infinitely to children 'whose needs, dispositions, aptitudes or circumstances require particularly perceptive and expert teaching and, in some cases, additional support' (OFSTED, 2012, p. 6).

Vulnerability is not only expanding in formal policy arenas. When I worked with young unemployed 16-19-year-olds in the late 1970s, before moving into further and then higher education in the early 1980s to work with young people and adults described at that time as 'second chance learners', the labels or descriptors of vulnerability did not exist. Things could not be more different today. At all levels of the education system, even the most cursory appraisal of the language that educators use about students, and the language students use about themselves, reveals a huge change in cultural, popular and professional discourses and associated assumptions about motivation, resilience and ability. Overt references to 'vulnerable' learners now characterise whole groups and individuals, most notably in universities in relation to 'widening participation' and 'non-traditional' students. Intertwining with labels of 'at risk learners', 'learners with fragile identities', the 'disaffected, disengaged and hard to reach', 'people with fragmented lives and complex needs', 'low self-esteemers' and 'anxious learners', the language of vulnerability pervades social and educational policy, institutional systems and processes and everyday conversations among academics, teachers, parents and students.

Intertwined invariably with risk, harm and resilience, vulnerability is also enmeshed in academic research in science, security, health and social policy (see Furedi, 2008). In various areas of social science, highly influential arguments come from self-defined 'progressive' or 'radical' standpoints that resist the pathologisation of vulnerability as a problem or weakness, or as a target for punitive or repressive forms of state intervention, and, instead, see vulnerability as a way of thinking about social justice. Here the obvious existential dimension of human experience and identity, namely that we are vulnerable to death, at risk from illness, disability and material deprivation expands to encompass a much more diffuse 'precarity' created by late capitalism's dismantling of the 'conditions for living' and its wearing out of bodies and minds (see, for example, Paur et al., 2012; Fineman, 2008 and Goodley in Ecclestone and Goodley, 2014). Regarded as a contemporary political 'springboard', vulnerability resonates powerfully with older debates about social justice that shift calls for redistribution of resources from material ones to 'relational justice' through identity recognition and expanded interpretations of social and cultural capital that draw in 'emotional' and 'identity' capitals (e.g. Reay, 2012; Leathwood and Hey, 2009; Lewis, 2014 and Lewis et al., 2015).

Proliferating uses of vulnerability in policy, research, everyday institutional and personal life, and their integration with ideas about social justice, generate a mushrooming list of harms and risks deemed to make people vulnerable. Here, serious structural problems of poverty, unemployment, homelessness, oppression and inequality now lie on an expanding spectrum with mundane, commonplace experiences. For example, the unemployed are vulnerable to loss of confidence, low self-esteem and resilience; young women to body image issues; high-achieving students to stress and anxiety; working class or 'non-traditional' students to unfamiliar or oppressive forms of knowledge and assessment; children to social media bullying; young men to pornography; university students to low grades and critical feedback about their work and so on. While policy, research and everyday invocations of vulnerability and related understandings of risk and harm might acknowledge particular structural and material aspects such as poverty, unemployment, homelessness, inequality and oppression, these are invariably presented as a set of psycho-emotional causes and effects, remedies and responses.

As Ashley Frawley observes in her study of the rise of the happiness and wellbeing industry, these perspectives do not merely depict vulnerability as an inherent psychological state generated by the oppressions and inequalities of capitalism but as a state generated by social and economic progress per se. One effect is a 'morality of low expectations', among governments and citizens alike, that downplays material expectations and elevates other dimensions to wellbeing and quality of life (see Frawley, 2014). In this context, general notions of wellbeing are portrayed as a psycho-emotional state that perhaps also incorporates spiritual dimensions. Other standpoints go further, presenting vulnerability as the 'demonstration of a lack of worldliness and the possession of an undiscriminating and individual naiveté in conducting the tough business of life' (Frankburg et al. in Frawley 2014, p. 101). In a related vein, British commentator Will Hutton expands the definition of vulnerability even more, regarding growing numbers of 'the hapless public' as not merely vulnerable to particular structural conditions or even to a seemingly inexorable widening of everyday harms, risks and threats. Instead, he argues, most people 'do not possess the mental equipment to be rational about why and what they choose' nor know how to be happy (Hutton, in Frawley, 2014, p. 134). Vulnerability becomes enmeshed with irrationality and neuroticism.

These powerful psychological emphases in understandings of vulnerability are fuelled by, and reinforce, calls to raise 'awareness' of mental health and to de-stigmatise people 'coming out' with problems. Here the World Health Organization's apocryphal proclamation that mental illness is the world's biggest health crisis, together with revisions to criteria for defining psychological disorders in each new edition of the *Diagnostic Statistical Manual* have inflated clinical diagnoses to an all-time high (see Harwood and Allen, 2014). Mirroring and intersecting with this proliferation of policy, academic and everyday uses of vulnerability, formal diagnoses and mental health awareness-raising have expanded the informal meanings we now attach to stress, anxiety, depression, abuse, trauma and recovery. As with vulnerability, references to mental illness are recast as mental health problems or, even more vaguely, mental health 'issues', in a spectrum ranging from serious conditions to everyday feelings and responses.

Changing the subject of education

Culturally and socially, then, very diverse concerns from equally diverse sources inform the framing of people as vulnerable to create an iterative relationship between policy, practice and everyday interactions. One outcome over the past fifteen years or so is the rise of specialist or targeted interventions and support systems in family, welfare and social work, youth justice, schools, colleges, adult education centres, universities and workplaces (Ecclestone and Hayes, 2009; Davies, 2015; Brown, 2015). In all these settings, specialist interventions parallel a lucrative, eclectic market of generic or universal approaches. These define risks and vulnerabilities extremely widely before offering strategies for developing the necessary skills of 'positive motivation', resilience, mindfulness, mental toughness, 'positive thinking' and anxiety management. For example, students at the University of East Anglia can access the 'support' of therapy dogs when they feel anxious or depressed, while other universities have compulsory resilience classes for medical students and trainee teachers, online self-help groups, Cognitive Behavioural Therapy and stress management courses.

Both as a response to stressful institutional assessment and audit systems and a way of generating and monitoring the required targets and outputs, vague notions of vulnerability are now embedded in activities for personal development, reflective practice, performance appraisals and reviews.

Three specific examples illustrate the reach of vulnerability into formal university systems and processes. First, a university counselling services leaflet handed out during freshers' week at Edge Hill University in 2007 argued that:

> In Health Care, some people in the caring role at work can mean they are always seen in this role [...] and so it can become hard to attend to their own needs and feelings which may go unmet [...] [in their work] students are faced, sometimes on a daily basis, with loss [...] and this can make it doubly hard if they are dealing with their own losses, such as a relationship ending or bereavement [...]
>
> The pressures of life in schools dealing with the issues of young people can make considerable emotional and physical demands [...]
>
> Students [...] in the disciplines of Psychology, Sociology, or the Expressive Arts may find themselves re-examining areas of their lives which have previously seemed unproblematic to them.

(Edge Hill University Counselling Services, 2007)

In 2012, the University of Wolverhampton's Institute for Learning Enhancement criticised academic instructions for assessed work:

> Research shows that attainment levels can be associated with the quality of the assignment brief:

students report that unclear and unwieldy briefs produce learner anxiety: students spend days trying to decode the brief rather than getting down to the assignment.

University ethics committees are also highly influential in normalising extremely general definitions of actual or potential vulnerability, harm and risk, and in requiring formal strategies and responses. Such descriptors now apply to anyone taking part in research project interviews or observations, no matter what the subject content or type of participant. For example, an education doctoral student in my university recently had her ethics application returned because a reviewer deemed her assertion that there was no 'risk of psychological harm' in interviews with legal experts about lawyers' professional education to be inadequate; instead, she had to provide a lengthy explanation of the steps she would take to avoid psychological harm and deal with cases where it might arise. In another application, the reviewer added a note to the student's declaration that there were no potential or actual psychological harms in an auto-ethnography of her own long career working with 'at risk' children that alerted her to the possibility that deep and sustained personal reflection might be a risk to her own wellbeing.

More subtly, advocates of institutional systems, teaching and assessment methods and curriculum content designed around notions of inclusion, widening participation, student-centred learning and student 'voice' argue that exposure of the psycho-social effects and causes of inequality is a key source of recognition and therefore integral to social justice. From this perspective, educators need better insights into the ways in which non-traditional students live inequalities emotionally and psychologically, and the effects of these on learning identities, approaches to learning and educational outcomes (see Reay, 2012; Leathwood and Hey, 2009; Lewis, 2014). As a key theme in these educational arguments, vulnerability resonates with concerns that downplaying the role of emotional dimensions of learning in favour of rational and cognitive ones reinforces dualism between the intellectual and emotional (see Beard et al. 2007). Others argue that portrayals of the emotional and vulnerable subject as 'diminished' are 'othering', masculinist, elitist and ableist (see Leathwood and Hey, 2009; Goodley in Ecclestone and Goodley, 2014). Both strands of these influential arguments emerge from and reinforce long-running political and philosophical scepticism that the rational, autonomous 'ideal citizen' is unrealistic, anachronistic, a myth or fiction and, in its dominant western, male, heteronormative and able-bodied forms, fundamentally oppressive (see Malik, 2001; Heartfield, 2002).

Endorsed as a focus for 'progressive' educational politics, the universally vulnerable subject combines with other calls to shift priorities for resources and expertise towards psychological interpretations of students' needs. For example, some academics argue that designers and implementers of student assessment should explore and respond to 'non-traditional' students' expectations and experiences (Cramp et al. 2012). In the light of these ideas, there is a corresponding shift in curriculum knowledge across the whole education system towards the personal, local and affective. This also resonates powerfully with a wider tendency to regard traditional subjects as creating adversity, risk and harm in their own right. Here students, especially those categorised as 'non-traditional', are seen as burdened by their elitist, irrelevant, over-rational demands and/or their inherent elitism, racism, sexism and colonialism (see Winter, 2014; White, 2004). More mundanely, some educators seem to see students as simply bored and disengaged by the irrelevance of curriculum subjects to everyday life, generating a popular associated view that education should be a skills-based preparation for contemporary real life.

Although not all these disaffections with traditional knowledge, teaching and assessment methods intend to erode controversial or difficult content in lectures or seminars, they are linked inextricably to the wider climate of concerns about vulnerability. This creates not just the examples of trigger warnings and bans mentioned above but also a growing tendency towards small, almost unconscious, incidents of self-censorship and self-editing and a growing sense of hesitancy in how we teach, assess and tutor students, interact with colleagues at all levels, and do our research. As Bill Durodié argues, this is already a strong feature of teaching in both schools and universities, reflected in a seeming growing reluctance from teachers to discuss difficult, contentious topics or to make value-judgments about students' views (Durodié, 2016). The overall effect is that an ethos of not wanting to upset or pressure people, to avoid difficulty, discomfort or controversy and to regard people as vulnerable to being influenced adversely by strong views, comes to permeate everyday university life.

The erosion of academic freedom

As other chapters in this book show, how we think about academic freedom cannot be divorced from freedom of expression in wider society. In a context of government proposals to limit expression of certain radical views and to require universities to play an active role in detecting vulnerability to radicalisation, school-based initiatives with this aim set stark precedents for academic freedom (UK Government, 2011, 2015). For example, the Labour government's 'Learning Together to Be Safe: a toolkit to help schools contribute to the prevention of violent extremism' (DCSF, 2008), requires teachers to detect 'vulnerability to radicalisation' among young Muslims. As well as offering a simplistic, casual and far-reaching elision of vulnerability with mental health, the Prevent Duty presents the vulnerability and wellbeing both of young people themselves, and that of the wider population they might threaten if they become 'vulnerable to radicalisation', as the key concern of the strategy. It then offers 'indicators' that identify wide ranging characteristics of many young people driven by: 'a search for answers to questions about identity, faith and belonging [...] the desire for 'adventure' and excitement [...] a desire to enhance the self-esteem of the individual and promote their 'street cred'; [...] identification with a charismatic individual and attraction to a group which can offer identity, social network and support' (DCSF, p. 17). A psycho-emotional interpretation of vulnerability is integral to examples of 'extremist narratives' and possible 'psychological hooks' that may increase an individual's 'vulnerability' to extremist engagement, followed by the catch-all category of 'relevant mental health issues'.

Through its targeting of motivations typical of any young people who seek new ways of thinking about the world and perhaps hope to change it, this intervention casts the mental wellbeing of all young British Muslims as a problem, thereby rendering them as 'appropriate objects for state intervention and surveillance' (Coppock and McGovern, 2014, p. 242). Expanding surveillance is not the only salient point for discussion here about links between vulnerability and academic freedom. Amid crisis discourses of mental illness, the Prevent Duty's sweeping reference to 'mental health issues' draws in attitudes and views merely different to the mainstream or openly critical of the existing social order as signs of 'vulnerability' to radicalisation. Significantly, the Prevent Duty's recourse to psycho-emotional vulnerability and its calls for early intervention and 'support' are normalised by targeted and generic programmes that are, as I observed above, already commonplace in educational settings. Yet, while the Prevent Duty's depiction of subjects lacking any rational capacity for political views, however unpalatable those views might be, is much more far-reaching, this can be seen as a logical outcome of a broader climate of vulnerability and schools' and universities' responses to it. This legislation, together with a concern that people are vulnerable to knowledge per se, softens universities up for overt bans and other constraints on the grounds of students' psycho-emotional vulnerability (see also Durodié, 2016).

It is important to reiterate that initiatives such as the Prevent Duty and other overt attempts to constrain what can and cannot be said or discussed (such as trigger warnings and bans on debates or speakers) are only one type of threat to academic freedom. Prevent cannot therefore be divorced from insidious erosions that emerge when human subjects are regarded as psycho-emotionally at risk, inherently irrational, hapless and naïve, facing growing adversities yet unaware of their damaging psychological causes and effects, and lacking effective strategies for dealing with them.

In a culture where concerns about vulnerability are embedded in fears about a crisis of mental health, long running calls for educators to explore and discuss emotional barriers to learning and achievement, and to regard the curriculum as inherently problematic, take on a new significance. For example, it is hardly surprising that more students and parents use psycho-emotional vulnerability to make tutors and lecturers sympathetic to difficulties and willing to reduce their demands. A recent study of 'emotional strategising' by students wishing to gain concessions and sympathetic treatment from lecturers highlights numerous examples of this creeping trend (Bartram, 2015). There has also been a rapid increase in formal requests for mental health problems to be seen as grounds for mitigation, fuelling fears that changes to disability legislation will require universities to fund more support for psycho-emotional needs or risk litigation on the grounds that lack of support hindered academic success.

In this climate, the Edge Hill example above, which first appeared in *The Dangerous Rise of Therapeutic Education* (Ecclestone and Hayes, 2009), is prescient. In presenting counselling as a desirable response to the psycho-emotional 'risks' created by exposure to ideas and difficult experiences, ideas and knowledge themselves became threatening. Today, the strengthening of this view amid various forms of self-imposed and external censoring in everyday university life enables Prevent's depiction of students as easily influenced by ideas, incapable of any real rational capacity to discern and make choices about those ideas to have a powerful purchase (see also Durodié, 2016).

Practical resistances

Developments explored in this chapter raise questions about how academics, support staff, institutional managers and students who are concerned about the rise of the vulnerable human and curriculum subject might respond. We can resist the language of vulnerability and criticise those who trivialise psycho-emotional problems for their own advantage. We could point out the danger of endorsing a self-fulfilling prophecy of need, where a highly contagious social construction turns everyday mundane experiences and relationships, some of which can sometimes be difficult, troubling, stressful or anxiety inducing, into potential mental health time-bombs. We can research the trends discussed here empirically to see what evidence there is for the arguments presented in this paper.

More practically, we can become Orwellian experts in Newspeak, perhaps by rewriting publicity for support services and introductions for new students to erase the language of vulnerability and the active soliciting of requests for students to regard help for anxiety and stress as normal, routine entitlements. We can resist calls to expand support and counselling services, discuss where scarce resources for support should go and perhaps be more discerning about sick notes and mitigation. We can challenge an erosion of crucial distinctions between mental health and wellbeing that, as the Chief Medical Officer argues in her 2013 report on public health priorities, hinders clear assessments of the extent of mental illness, the establishment of clear evidence for intervention and decisions about how to allocate scarce specialist resources for genuine need (Davies, 2013).

Finally, despite the unpopularity of belief in the potential of the rational, agentic human subject, there needs to be stronger advocacy of a curriculum based on 'powerful' subject knowledge, namely knowledge that 'is cognitively superior to that needed for daily life' (Young, 2013, p. 118; see also Furedi, 2011; Ecclestone and Hayes, 2009).

Yet not only do all these proposals seem to be a minority standpoint in the current climate of higher education, there is also danger of regarding overt support interventions, psycho-emotional training and coaching as the main threat to academic freedom. I would argue that everyday changes to social and academic relations that are framed through the lens of vulnerability are more pervasive and difficult to discern and discuss, and therefore perhaps more damaging. Questions about the impact of vulnerability and how to address them therefore remain. Does attention to vulnerability create a self-fulfilling prophecy that diminishes expectations about students' capacity for agency, robust debate and academic challenge? Does the rise of vulnerability make it difficult to differentiate between serious and trivial claims and to allocate scarce resources? How are views about academic freedom affected when curriculum subjects and even educators themselves come to be seen as risks and threats, as new sources of vulnerability?

In considering these questions, it is important to recognise that student presentations of vulnerability are not merely put on or socially constructed. Instead, outside those making obviously trivial or cynical claims and those with serious problems, more and more people do experience everyday life, relationships and education itself as ever-present sources of distress.

Serious causes for concern about the creeping impact of the psychologically and emotionally vulnerable, irrational and anxious subject on what and how we teach, the ways in which we relate to students and colleagues and on academic confidence and freedom, therefore remain.

References

Bartram, B. (2015) 'Emotion as a Student Resource in Higher Education' in *British Journal of Educational Studies*. (63) 1, pp. 67–84.

Beard, C., Clegg, S. and Smith, A. (2007) 'Acknowledging the affective in higher education' in *British Educational Research Journal*. (33) 2 pp. 235–252.

Brown, K. (2015) *Vulnerability and young people: care and control in social policy*. Bristol: The Policy Press.

Coppock, V. and McGovern, M. (2014) 'Dangerous Minds'? Deconstructing Counter-Terrorism Discourse, Radicalisation and the 'Psychological Vulnerability' of Muslim Children and Young People in Britain' in *Children and Society*. (28) pp. 242–256.

Cramp, A., Lamond, C., Coleyshaw, L. and Beck, S. (2012) 'Empowering or disabling? Emotional reactions to assessment amongst part-time adult students' in *Teaching in Higher Education*. (17) 5 pp. 509–521.

Davies, S. C. (2014) *Annual Report of the Chief Medical Officer 2013, Public Mental Health Priorities: Investing in the Evidence*. London: Department of Health.

Davies, W. (2015) *The happiness industry: how government and big business sold us happiness and well-being*. London: Verso.

Durodié, B. (2016) 'Securitising education to prevent terrorism or losing direction?' in *British Journal of Educational Studies*. (In press).

Ecclestone, K. and Goodley, D. (2014) 'Political and educational springboard or straitjacket? Theorising post/humanist subjects in an age of vulnerability' in *Discourse: Studies in the Cultural Politics of Education*. DOI: 10.1080/01596306.2014.927112.

Ecclestone, K. and Lewis, L. (2014) 'Interventions for emotional well-being in educational policy and practice: Challenging discourses of 'risk' and 'vulnerability'' in *Journal of Education Policy*. (24) 1 pp. 192–214.

Ecclestone, K. and Hayes, D. (2009) *The Dangerous Rise of Therapeutic Education.* London: Routledge.

Fineman, M. (2008) 'The vulnerable subject and the responsive state' in *Yale Journal of Law and Feminism,* (20) 1 pp. 1–22.

Frawley, A. (2014). *The semiotics of happiness: the rhetorical beginnings of a social problem.* London: Bloomsbury.

Furedi, F. (2004) *Therapy culture: Cultivating vulnerability in an uncertain age.* London: Routledge.

Harwood, V. and Allan, J. (2014) *Psychopathology at school: theorizing education and mental disorder.* London: Routledge.

H. M. Government. (2011) *Prevent Strategy.* Available at: https:// www.gov.uk/government/uploads/system/uploads/attachment_ data/file/97976/prevent- strategy-review.pdf (accessed 03/04/16).

H. M. Government. (2015) *Prevent Duty Guidance.* Available at: http://www.legislation.gov.uk/ukdsi/2015/9780111133309/pdfs/u kdsiod_9780111133309_en.pdf (accessed 03/04/16).

Hume, M. (2015) *Trigger warning: is the fear of giving offence killing free speech?* London: William Collins.

Leathwood, C. and Hey, V. (2009) 'Gender/ed discourses and emotional subtexts: theorising emotion in UK higher education' in *Teaching and Learning in Higher Education,* (14) 4 pp. 429–440.

Lewis, L. (2014). 'Responding to the mental health and well-being agenda in adult and community learning' in *Research in Post-Compulsory Education* (19) 4 pp. 357–377.

Lewis, L., Ecclestone, K., Spandler, H. and Tew, J. (2013). 'Mutual recovery and mental health in adult and community education and community arts' *Project in the Arts and Humanities Research Council Connected Communities Programme,* University of Wolverhampton.

Malik, K. (2001) *Man, Beast or Zombie?* London: Weidenfield.

McLaughlin, K. (2011) *Surviving Identity: Vulnerability and the Psychology of Recognition.* London: Routledge.

McLeod, J. (2012) 'Vulnerability and the neo-liberal youth citizen: a view from Australia' in *Comparative Education,* (48) 1 pp. 11–26.

Office for Standards in Education (2012) *Good practice in creating an inclusive school,* London: Department for Education.

Paur, J. (2012) 'Precarity talk: a virtual roundtable with Lauren Berlant, Judith Butler, Borjan Cvejic, Isabell Lorey, Jasbir Paur, Ana Vujan, in *The Drama Review,* (56) 4 pp. 163–177.

Reay, D. (2005) 'Beyond consciousness: the psychic landscape of social class', in *Sociology* (39) 5 pp. 911–928.

White, J. (2004) (Ed.) *Rethinking the School Curriculum*, London: Routledge.

Winter, C. (2014) 'Curriculum knowledge, justice, relations: The Schools' White Paper (2010) in England', in *Journal of Philosophy of Education*, (48) 2 pp. 276–292.

Warning: On Campus, a Fear of Words and Ideas

Jenny Jarvie

Every age has its doomsayers who warn of the dangers of reading. In 370 BC, Socrates worried that the spread of literacy would weaken readers' memory and mislead them to think that they had wisdom when they had only information. A book, he told Phaedrus, could never capture 'an intelligent word graven in the soul of the learner' (in Jowett, trans. p. 485). More than 2,000 years later, Gustave Flaubert depicted Emma in *Madame Bovary*, 'her hands dirty with books from old lending libraries' (pt. 1, ch. 6), so susceptible to the fantasies of novels that she struggled to reconcile romantic fiction with real life.

Today the act of reading has become ever more fraught, as a new generation scours both the spoken and written word, honing in on any potential for psychological harm. At universities across the US, many students have come to approach books and lectures with trepidation, demanding 'trigger warnings' on epic narrative poems that have been studied for centuries and novels long considered suitable material in high schools.

The practice, which began on the Internet as a gesture of sensitivity, has become fiercely contested as students have called for alerts on Ovid's *Metamorphoses* (rape and sexual assault), F. Scott Fitzgerald's *The Great Gatsby* (suicide, domestic abuse and graphic violence), and William Shakespeare's *The Merchant of Venice* (anti-Semitism). Even Chinua Achebe's *Things Fall Apart*, the modern African novel hailed for its searing account of Western colonisation, has been flagged for its depictions of racism, religious persecution, and violence (Jarvie, 2014).

American campuses have not reached *Fahrenheit 451* territory, with books outlawed and stowed under pillows and in air-conditioning ducts. Yet it would be naïve to shrug off the requests for disclaimers on key cultural touchstones of human knowledge, with the word 'trigger' suggesting material so disturbing it could cause severe flashbacks or panic attacks. Far from an insignificant pop fad, the trigger warning marks a notable shift in students' relationship with words and ideas, one that explicitly prioritises caution over exploration and emotional reaction over rational engagement.

Such alerts are part of a burgeoning impulse of hyper-protection on campus. In the ongoing quest for building 'safe spaces' and calling out 'microaggressions', more academics and students are approaching the university as a place of infinite risk.

This focus on emotional harm, rather than intellectual curiosity, poses a challenge to higher education's traditional mission of free and reasoned enquiry. As students are viewed as more fragile, and words are seen as more dangerous, the idea of the university as a hub of intellectual exploration and rational thought – a place dedicated, above all, to the pursuit of knowledge – is in question. As the American Association of University Professors (AAUP) has noted, trigger warnings threaten longstanding ideas of academic freedom. 'The presumption that students need to be protected rather than challenged in a classroom is at once infantilizing and anti-intellectual,' its committee on academic freedom stated in a 2014 report. 'It makes comfort a higher priority than intellectual engagement' (AAUP, 01/08/14).

The university has a special interest in encouraging free enquiry. Its goal, at least historically, has been to promote the study of traditional and new ideas, advance the sum of human knowledge and cultivate the intellectual development of all who enter its walls. It would be a mistake, however, to understand the trigger warning simply as a populist interloper, an example of mainstream therapy and self-help culture invading the hallowed halls of education. Actually, the state of high alert on university campuses comes from within: trigger warnings are the logical culmination of a decades-long academic preoccupation with vulnerability and hypersensitivity to language in college classrooms.

Stretching the concept of emotional harm

The idea of triggering dates back to World War I, when psychologists began to develop theories of shell shock after treating soldiers exposed to frontline combat who exhibited extreme physical reactions, such as impaired hearing and loss of balance. In 1980, post-traumatic stress disorder (PTSD) was recognised as a distinct mental disorder afflicting those who had experienced combat, terrorist attacks, car wrecks, natural disasters and sexual or physical assault. About half of the population undergoes such a traumatic event, according to the National Center for PTSD, yet only seven to eight per cent are estimated to experience the disorder.

Since PTSD entered the mainstream lexicon, the concept of psychological harm has expanded, moving beyond extreme trauma to microaggressions, a term first coined by Harvard psychiatrist, Chester M. Pierce, in the 1970s, and popularised more recently by Derald Wing Sue, a psychology professor at Columbia University. In *Microagressions in Everyday Life*, Wing Sue argues that casual verbal and behavioural slights and snubs, no matter the intent, can have devastating, long-term consequences. Not only can they 'assail the self-esteem' and 'produce anger and frustration', but they can 'deplete' physical health, 'shorten life expectancy, and deny minority populations equal access and opportunity in education, employment, and health care' (Wing Sue, 2010, p. 6).

This emphasis on subtle forms of harm extends to other academic fields, too. Sociologists, for example, have increasingly honed in on culture as a form of domination. In 1979, French social theorist Pierre Bourdieu developed the concept of 'symbolic power' to describe the implicit, almost unconscious, forms of cultural and social domination that operate within routine language and customs. Symbolic power, Bourdieu argued, can hold more sway than overt forms of physical and economic power because it is ingrained in everyday, supposedly common sense individual habits and thought.

This stretching of the boundaries of psychological harm and intense scrutiny of cultural power has had a significant impact on campus language and behaviour, with activists increasingly working with administrators to draw up faculty speech guidelines and codes of conduct. At the University of California, for example, a 2014 training handout, 'Tool: Recognizing Microaggressions and the Messages They Send', instructs faculty to identify any language that could be deemed a microaggression. Examples include asking a student 'Where are you from?' or describing America as a 'land of opportunity'.

As Bradley Campbell and Jason Manning argue in a 2015 paper, 'Microaggression and Moral Cultures', a new moral culture of victimhood has emerged in which individuals and groups display extreme sensitivity to minor or indirect slights and handle conflicts through complaints to authorities. The result is a constant escalation of disputes as people compete for status as victims, or as defenders of victims. The more gains made in education, law and the workplace, the more outrage seems to be generated by ever smaller offences. 'The goalposts shift,' as Jonathan Haidt wrote on his blog, The Righteous Mind, 'allowing participants to maintain a constant level of anger and constant level of perceived victimization' (07/09/15).

It is hardly surprising, then, that students who have been taught that they are vulnerable to an ever-expanding assault of subtle harms now scrutinise classroom discussion and academic texts for potentially painful material. Amid a state of high alert about student risk, universities find themselves in the surreal position of fostering a more precautionary, one-dimensional and emotional approach to learning, anxiously vetting words and ideas that might cause psychological pain.

In an era of growing faculty insecurity, with more than half of instructors working part-time and three quarters lacking tenure, many lecturers avoid expressing anything that might remotely lead to offence. 'Boat-rocking isn't just dangerous, it's suicidal,' one instructor, writing under the pseudonym Edward Schlosser, wrote for *Vox* magazine; 'Teachers limit their lessons to things they know won't upset anybody' (03/06/15). In *Psychology Today*, Peter Gray, a research professor of psychology at Boston College, noted that fear of agitating students has become so acute that some members of faculty avoid assigning low grades 'because of the subsequent emotional crises they would have to deal with in their offices' (22/09/15).

Warnings: from the internet to the classroom

The 'trigger warning' first emerged on the Internet as a way of moderating chatrooms and message boards for the vulnerable and mentally ill. In the early days of online support and self-help groups, the rationale was to give traumatised or sensitive readers – for example, a rape victim, or someone with an eating disorder – a heads-up before posting particularly graphic content that might lead to distressing memories, flashbacks, or panic attacks.

Gradually, Internet users began to conflate trauma with discomfort, affixing the term to a bewildering array of topics, from sex and childbirth to fat-shaming and transphobia, even insects and tiny holes. In 2010, sex blogger Susannah Breslin took to her blog, True/Slant, to accuse feminists of applying trigger warnings 'like a Southern cook applies Pam cooking spray to an overused non-stick frying pan' 13/04/10). When students began to demand trigger warnings in the classroom, traditionally a place for in-depth study and critical analysis, some lecturers agreed, largely because arguments were framed in terms of safety.

In *The New York Times*, Bailey Loverin, a student at the University of California, Santa Barbara, argued that 'without a trigger warning, a survivor might black out, become hysterical or feel forced to leave the room' (19/05/14).

There is, however, little academic consensus that a system of warnings can help victims of major trauma or trivial slights. Actually, alerts can be counterproductive, argues Richard J. McNally, Professor of Psychology at Harvard University and an expert on anxiety disorders. Not only can they underestimate the resilience of the majority of trauma survivors, but they can dissuade those who have developed PTSD from recovering: 'Systematic exposure to triggers and the memories they provoke is the most effective means of overcoming the disorder' (McNally, 20/05/15).

Even with scant evidence that trigger warnings protect students, support for the device has grown: a 2015 survey of 800 US college students found that 63 per cent favoured requiring instructors to use such alerts (McLaughlin & Associates, 26/10/15). Discussions continue to rage in classrooms, faculty meetings, and newspapers, with each side accusing the other of over-reacting. Those who oppose trigger warnings claim alerts encourage students to over-emphasise the risk of words and build on an exaggerated sense of victimhood. Supporters, in turn, counter that alerts are a relatively straightforward gesture of compassion, and the backlash is a panicked, hysterical response to perceived political correctness.

Not everyone who advocates for trigger warnings agrees on how they should be applied. Some academics, after issuing alerts, do not allow students to skip readings or lectures (Manne, 2015), while others invite students to avoid potentially upsetting content

(Marshall, 2014; Johnston, 2014). Many instructors who issue content warnings resist mandatory alerts, insisting they should be free to exercise their own judgement. 'There is already too much threat to academic freedom at the moment because of top-down interference from overreaching administrators,' Kate Manne, an assistant professor of philosophy at Cornell University, wrote in *The New York Times* (19/09/15).

Yet even voluntary use of trigger warnings poses a challenge for academic freedom, a concept that, as the AAUP's 1915 *Declaration* notes, has traditionally involved not just the freedom of the teacher to teach (*Lehrfreiheit*), but the freedom of the student to learn (*Lernfreiheit*). As professors impose blanket warnings on classroom material in the name of protection, they discourage students from engaging openly and rationally with the text.

Comfort vs. exploration

Some professors who have adopted trigger warnings push back against the idea that the device is anti-intellectual. For Manne, the point is not to deter anyone from reading or engaging with material, but to nurture a more productive learning environment. 'It's not about coddling anyone,' she argued, 'it's about enabling everyone's rational engagement' (19/09/15).

Logically, it might seem a stretch to argue that imposing warnings on certain words and ideas due to their potential to inflict emotional harm is intellectual. By definition, an intellectual environment promotes rational and intelligent thought and upholds knowing as distinguished from feeling and experience. Yet the argument that alerts prepare students for rational discussion echoes key tenets of modern educational theory, popularised by bell hooks's idea of 'engaged pedagogy', in rejecting the traditional dualism of thinking versus feeling, and encouraging instructors to embrace a more nurturing and therapeutic role in the classroom. 'Our work is not merely to share information but to share in the intellectual and spiritual growth of our students,' hooks argued in *Teaching to Transgress*. 'To teach in a manner that respects and cares for the souls of our students is essential if we are to provide the necessary conditions where learning can most deeply and intimately begin' (hooks, 1994, p. 13).

Increasingly, scholars draw on personal narrative and first-person experience, rather than logic and rhetoric. In a typical example, a recent UCLA diversity training document recommends that academics use personal narrative 'to concretise subject matter and make connections between classroom and life experience' (Garibay, 2014, p. 17). Another proclaims: 'A learning environment where all feel safe, valued, and respected is necessary for students to achieve and demonstrate their full potential' (Garibay, 2015, p. 3).

How does one define safety in an era when students have an inflated sense of risk? Assuming students and academics are not physically attacking each other in class, it seems reasonable to infer that safety, in the context of the learning environment, is intellectual safety, a concept that is incompatible with challenging students to question their beliefs and strengthen their arguments. Trigger warnings do not seem to ease tension in the classroom, so much as frame students' experience, preventing them from approaching material spontaneously and setting expectations that classrooms value caution over exploration. Instead of engaging in considered and reasoned critique, warnings prompt students to approach books and lectures through the narrow prism of personal experience and emotional hurt. The idea of triggering in the academic setting – understanding words as devices that activate a simple mechanism – reinforces knee-jerk, anti-intellectual attitudes to language and human response. While some words or ideas may provoke extreme responses, they are not, in themselves, harmful. Two women who have suffered sexual assault, for example, might react completely differently to Toni Morrison's novel Beloved or Alexander Pope's mock-heroic poem, *The Rape of the Lock*. In issuing broad warnings to entire classes of students, instructors undermine the dynamism and complexity of language, and play down the nuance and variety of human interpretation.

Once a lecturer issues trigger warnings, where does he or she stop? Agreeing to one student's claim of harm can invite objections to other kinds of content; setting in motion an expectation that faculty will accede to any suggestion of offence. Imagine a professor attaches the following warning to Tolstoy's *Anna Karenina*: 'Trigger warning: suicide.' How should the instructor respond if a student claims to be disturbed by the novel's portrayal of train accidents or unhappy marriage, difficult childbirth or consumption?

As Greg Lukianoff notes in *Freedom From Speech*: 'When students take advantage of a psychological term developed to help those traumatised in the ghastly trenches of World War I to justify being protected from *The Great Gatsby* [...] it becomes clear that there is virtually no limit to the demands that will be made if we universalise an expectation of intellectual comfort' (Lukianoff, 2015, p. 57).

Already, the intense focus on protecting students from emotional harm is encouraging some to push their war against words and images beyond warnings. When speech is stigmatised as emotionally threatening or wounding, attention tends to focus on stamping it out and containing it, rather than subjecting it to rational scrutiny. As Jeannie Suk, a law professor at Harvard University, recounted in a 2014 article for *The New Yorker*: after showing the 2003 documentary film, *Capturing the Friedmans*, some of her students urged her to use trigger warnings, while another argued that the film was so traumatising it should not have been shown at all.

Academic assault on words

Critics of trigger warnings are fond of bemoaning the new coddled generation of students, yet this is no straightforward inter-generational battle. In pushing the idea that words are intrinsically harmful, a form of violence in and of themselves, trigger warnings are the logical continuation of decades of academic theory on language. During the 1970s and 1980s, feminist theorists played a crucial role in breaking down the traditional distinction between actions and words, stressing a continuum of violence in their work against sexual harassment and pornography. Catharine MacKinnon, the radical feminist legal theorist, claimed that pornography constructs social reality and defines the treatment of women. 'Men treat women as who they see women being', she argued, 'pornography constructs who that is' (MacKinnon, 1987, p. 148). As Jonathan Rauch notes, MacKinnon implies 'not that pornography *causes* hurt, but that it *is* hurt' and that 'it *is* violence:

specifically, it is *group* violence against women' (Rauch, 1993, p. 17).

This insistence on the fundamental violence of words and images significantly alters the way we understand and interact with books and films, objectifying them as harmful rather than subject to complex patterns of intention and interpretation. The insistence on a word's harm defies scrutiny; whatever the intent, the focus is on the reader who perceives it as hurtful or distressing.

During the 1980s, the regulation of words and images was the subject of much disagreement between feminists. 'Are our new censors attempting, under the guise of feminism, to reinforce our culture's age-old tradition of paternalism – of treating women like infants?' asked Karen DeCrow, a former President of the National Organization for Women, in a 1985 edition of *Penthouse* (Denfeld, 1995, pp. 115–116). The more censorious brand of feminism, however, went on to make inroads in law and higher education. In 1980, the US Equal Employment Opportunity Commission determined that speech in the workplace constitutes sexual harassment if words create an 'intimidating, hostile or offensive' working environment. Throughout the 1990s, universities across the US implemented speech codes that defined harassment even more broadly. As therapeutic notions of society gained ground in academia, as well as popular culture, anxiety about the harmful effects of words grew.

In 2014, Jeannie Suk, the Harvard law professor, raised concern that some students had begun to ask lecturers not to teach rape law. One colleague, she wrote in *The New Yorker,* was asked not to use the word 'violate' in class to avoid 'triggering' distress (15/12/14). The insistence that teachers protect students from experiencing pain or offence, Suk argued, was impeding students' ability to 'engage productively and analytically' on critical aspects of the curriculum. 'Many students and teachers appear to be absorbing a cultural signal that real and challenging discussion of sexual misconduct is too risky to undertake – and that the risk is of a traumatic injury analogous to sexual assault itself' (15/12/14).

At Northwestern University, the aversion to challenging discussion resulted in a protest march against a film professor who wrote an article on student-professor dating. One student said she'd had a 'very visceral reaction' to Laura Kipnis' article in *The Chronicle of Higher Education*; another called it 'terrifying'. Before long, administrators sent Kipnis a letter informing her that she was the subject of a formal investigation due to student complaints that her essay had violated Title IX, the federal law that prohibits sex discrimination in education. 'It's astounding how aggressive students' assertions of vulnerability have gotten in the past few years,' Kipnis noted in another article, 'My Title IX Inquisition', for *The Chronicle of Higher Education*, 'Emotional discomfort is regarded as equivalent to material injury, and all injuries have to be remediated' (29/09/15).

Building a case for the robust student

Some critics claim the modern hyper-regulation of language marks a resurgence of political correctness, but calls for trigger warnings come not just from left-leaning students, but from those with conservative and religious sensibilities, too. The impulse for protection from words that traumatise, offend or fail to validate students' identity is more a form of emotional than political correctness, with language monitored in the name of personal sensitivity.

Issuing more warnings, and drawing up longer lists of what others can and cannot say, is unlikely to improve dialogue or reduce conflict. Instead, it only seems to undermine students' resilience, encouraging them to think they cannot cope with relatively minor setbacks. In *The Atlantic*, Greg Lukianoff and Jonathan Haidt have suggested that a campus that coddles students and encourages them to police each other's speech could have a detrimental impact on students' mental health, teaching them to 'think pathologically' (01/09/15). 'We have raised a generation of young people who have not been given the opportunity to learn how to solve their own problems,' Peter Gray, professor of psychology at Boston College, wrote in *Psychology Today*. 'They have not been given the opportunity to get into trouble and find their own way out, to experience failure and realise they can survive it, to be called bad names by others and learn how to respond without adult intervention' (22/09/15).

Inspiring a more robust generation of students, however, is tricky. As the trigger warning has become a flashpoint in the culture wars, many balk at criticising students. 'Getting angry at kids who leave lectures on rape is as useless as it is politically incoherent,' Elizabeth Bruenig argued in *The New Republic*. 'What is the proper response to students who wish to exit voluntary lectures and go someplace else? Should they be forced to stay?' (25/03/15).

Of course, the solution is not to get mad at students who leave lectures on rape, or coerce them to remain in their seats. Nor is it to defer to students, whatever they demand. Bruenig makes the case that 'colleges will – and should! – remain loci of experimental politics and their expressions' (25/03/15), but a precautionary approach to words and ideas represents a limited starting point for academic experimentalism. As the AAUP noted in 1915, the university performs a unique role as an 'intellectual experiment station, where new ideas may germinate', as well as a 'conservator of all genuine elements of value in the past thought and life of mankind which are not in the fashion of the moment' (AAUP, 1915, p. 297). Colleges built on warnings and safe spaces, with ongoing appeals to bureaucratic authority, are a dead end for genuine curiosity and exploration.

Some acknowledge the problem of campus overprotection, yet insist that students deserve sympathy: 'Rather than painting student activists as censors – trying to dictate who has to say what and when – we should instead see them as trapped in a corporate architecture of managing offense,' Fredrik deBoer argued in *The New York Times* (09/09/15). It is true that students have grown up in a system that encourages them to think of themselves as weak and depend on third parties to intervene on their behalf. Yet emphasising young people as victims of a censorious bureaucracy only seems to reinforce the idea that they are passive and fragile. It also lets academia off the hook for cultivating much of the modern focus on psychological harm and anxiety about language.

The challenge for academics who are concerned about the growing regulation of words and ideas in the university is simple, yet complicated: the values of free enquiry, logical thought and critical engagement are longstanding ideals that have already been fought for;

rediscovering them, however, is no small task in an educational climate that prioritises emotional safety and comfort. If academics do not defend the intellectual mission of the university, who will?

References

American Association of University Professors. (1915) *Appendix I: 1915 Declaration of Principles on Academic Freedom and Academic Tenure.* Available at: http://www.aaup.org/NR/rdonlyres/A6520A9D-0A9A-47B3-B550-C006B5B224E7/0/1915Declaration.pdf (accessed 18 /01/ 2016).

American Association of University Professors: Committee A on Academic Freedom and Tenure. (2014) *On Trigger Warnings.* Available at: http://www.aaup.org/report/trigger-warnings (accessed 18 /01/16).

Bourdieu, P. (1984) *Distinction: A Social Critique of the Judgement of Taste.* Cambridge: Harvard University Press.

Breslin, S. (2010) 'Trigger warning: this blog post may freak you the f*** out'. (13/04/10). Archived and available at: https://web. archive.org/web/20101130164709/http://trueslant.com/susannah breslin/2010/04/13/trigger-warning-this-blog-post-may-freak-you-the-f-out/ (accessed 19/01/16).

Bruenig, E. (2015) 'Stop Using College Students As Political Pawns' in *The New Republic*, (25/03/15). Available at: https:// newrepublic.com/article/121375/shulevitzs-new-york-times-essay-sparks-outrage (accessed 18 /01/16).

Campbell, B. & Manning, J. (2014) 'Microaggression and Moral Cultures' in *Comparative Sociology* (13), pp. 692–726.

deBoer, F. (2015) 'Why We Should Fear University, Inc.' in *The New York Times Magazine*, (09/09/15). Available at: http://www. nytimes.com/2015/09/13/magazine/why-we-should-fear-university-inc.html?_r=0 (accessed 18/01/16).

Denfeld, R. (1995) *The New Victorians: A Young Woman's Challenge to the Old Feminist Order.* New York: Grand Central Publishing.

Flaubert, G. (1958) *Madame Bovary.* New York: Pocket Books Inc.

Garibay, J. C. (2014) *Diversity in the Classroom. UCLA Diversity & Faculty Development.* Available at: https://faculty.diversity.ucla.edu/resources-for/teaching/diversity-in-the-classroom-booklet (accessed 18/01/16).

Garibay, J. C. (2015) *Creating a Positive Classroom Climate for Diversity in UCLA Diversity & Faculty Development.* Available at: https://faculty.diversity.ucla.edu/our-library/creating-a-positive-classroom-climate-for-diversity (accessed 18/01/16).

Gray, P. (2015) 'Declining Student Resilience: A Serious Problem for Colleges' in *Psychology Today,* (22/09/15). Available at: https://www.psychologytoday.com/blog/freedom-learn/201509/declining-student-resilience-serious-problem-colleges (accessed 18/01/16).

Haidt, J. (2015) 'Where microaggressions really come from: A sociological account' in *The Righteous Mind* (07/09/15). Available at: http://righteousmind.com/where-microaggressions-really-come-from/ (accessed 18/01/16).

hooks, b. (1994) *Teaching to Transgress: Education as the Practice of Freedom.* London: Routledge.

Jarvie, J. (2014) 'Trigger Happy' in *The New Republic,* (03/03/14). Available at: https://newrepublic.com/article/116842/trigger-warnings-have-spread-blogs-college-classes-thats-bad (accessed 18/01/16).

Johnston, A. (2014) 'Why I'll Add a Trigger Warning' in *Inside Higher Ed,* (29/05/14). Available at: https://www.insidehighered.com/views/2014/05/29/essay-why-professor-adding-trigger-warning-his-syllabus (accessed 18/01/16).

Jowett, B. (2013) Translation of Plato *Phaedrus* (15/01/13). Available at: http://www.gutenberg.org/files/1636/1636-h/1636-h.htm (accessed 03/04/16).

Kipnis, L. (2015) 'My Title IX Inquisition' in *The Chronicle of Higher Education, The Chronicle Review,* (29/05/15). Available at: http://laurakipnis.com/wp-content/uploads/2010/08/My-Title-IX-Inquisition-The-Chronicle-Review-.pdf (accessed 18/01/16).

Loverin, B. (2014) 'Trigger Warnings Encourage Free Thought and Debate' in *The New York Times,* (19/05/14). Available at: http://www.nytimes.com/roomfordebate/2014/05/19/restraint-of-expression-on-college-campuses/trigger-warnings-encourage-free-thought-and-debate (accessed 18/01/16).

Lukianoff, G. (2014) *Freedom From Speech.* New York: Encounter Books.

Lukianoff, G. & Haidt, J. (2015) 'The Coddling of the American Mind', *The Atlantic,* (01/09/15). Available at: http://www.theatlantic.com/magazine/archive/2015/09/the-coddling-of-the-american-mind/399356/ (accessed 18/01/16).

MacKinnon, C. (1987) *Feminism Unmodified: Discourse on Life and Law.* Cambridge MA: Harvard University Press.

Manne, K. (2015) 'Why I Use Trigger Warnings' in *The New York Times Sunday Review* (19 /09/15). Available at: http://www.nytimes.com/2015/09/20/opinion/sunday/why-i-use-trigger-warnings.html (accessed 18 /01/16).

Marshall, K. (2014) 'Trigger Warnings, Quentin Tarantino, and the College Classroom' in *Chronicle Vitae* (07/03/14). Available at: https://chroniclevitae.com/news/372-trigger-warnings-quentin-tarantino-and-the-college-classroom (accessed 18 /01/16).

McLaughlin & Associates. (2015) *National Undergraduate Study,* sponsored by The William F. Buckley, Jr. Program at Yale (26/10/15). Available at: http://mclaughlinonline.com/2015/10/26/the-william-f-buckley-jr-program-at-yale-almost-half-49-of-u-s-college-students-intimidated-by-professors-when-sharing-differing-beliefs-survey/ (accessed 03/04/16).

McNally, R. (2015) 'Hazard Ahead: The Problem with Trigger Warnings, According to the Research' in *Pacific Standard* (20/05/15). Available at: http://www.psmag.com/health-and-behavior/hazards-ahead-problem-trigger-warnings-according-research-81946 (accessed 18 /01/16).

National Center for PTSD (2015) 'How Common is PTSD?' U.S. Department of Veterans Affairs website. (Updated 20/08/15). Available at: http://www.ptsd.va.gov/public/PTSD-overview/basics/how-common-is-ptsd.asp (accessed 18 /01/16).

Rauch, J. (2013) *Kindly Inquisitors: The New Attacks on Free Thought.* Chicago: The University of Chicago Press.

Schlosser, E. (2015) 'I'm a liberal professor, and my liberal students terrify me' in *Vox*, (03/06/15). Available at: http://www.vox.com/2015/6/3/8706323/college-professor-afraid (accessed 18 /01/16).

Suk, J. (2014) 'The Trouble with Teaching Rape Law' in *The New Yorker*, (15/12/14). Available at: http://www.newyorker.com/news/news-desk/trouble-teaching-rape-law (accessed 18 /01/16).

University of California. (2014) *Tool: Recognizing Microaggressions and the Messages They Send.* Available at: http://www.ucop.edu/academic-personnel-programs/_files/seminars/Tool_Recognizing_Microaggressions.pdf (accessed 18/01/16).

Wing Sue, D. (2010) *Microaggressions in Everyday Life: Race, Gender, and Sexual Orientation.* Hoboken, NJ: John Wiley & Sons, Inc.

Je Suis Charlie, But…

Jane Weston Vauclair

This chapter will discuss two cases from 2015 of academic debate about the French satirical magazine *Charlie Hebdo* being cancelled due to safety concerns. Debates at Queen's University Belfast and the University of London in Paris were prevented from going ahead although, in the case of Belfast, the planned event was reinstated after media intervention. These moves to block academic discussion, I will argue, reflect specific ethical and global-local tensions within more widespread responses to the January 2015 assassinations of *Charlie Hebdo* journalists in Paris and their perceived implications for free speech.

January 2015 saw a tidal wave of solidarity for the French satirical newspaper *Charlie Hebdo* after two French Islamic gunmen carried out a massacre at its offices. Such global support was notably expressed through the widespread use of the Twitter hashtag #jesuischarlie. What had been a marginal satirical publication with a very limited readership – one indeed on the cusp of bankruptcy – was catapulted into a global arena where its specifically French satire was far from transparent or readily graspable, not least by non-Francophones. Its practices of caricaturing Islamic extremism in defence of secular Republican values swiftly became muddied by charges of racism –

something the newspaper had in fact always campaigned against – or at the very least, of crass cultural insensitivity. Richard Seymour of *Jacobin* magazine notably penned a piece on the day of the attacks calling the publication 'frankly racist' (Seymour, 07/01/15).

Two sets of tensions around *Charlie Hebdo's* satire swiftly emerged in the wake of the massacre. Both, I will argue, contributed to the publication lurching from being seen as a totem of free speech on the one hand, to a form of academic taboo on the other. This polarised perception of the magazine played out in the context of two UK French Studies events, one at Queen's University in Belfast and the other at the University of London Institute in Paris (ULIP). I was involved in these as a researcher on *Charlie Hebdo* and the French satirical press more generally. Both had worrying implications for academic freedom.

The first set of tensions were between the profoundly local nature of *Charlie Hebdo's* satire and the specific references needed to decode it, and the global scope of the attention it received in the wake of the killings. Commentators worldwide were being called upon to get to grips with a newspaper they often, at best, only had a passing familiarity with. *Charlie Hebdo's* cartoonist 'Luz' (Renald Luzier) evoked the crushing weight of such a burden for a newspaper which had been used to dismantling symbols through humour and which, he believed, would ill withstand becoming a symbol - or indeed a totem of freedom of expression – itself (Luz, 10/01/15). Such a contrast of scale was only amplified by the mammoth demonstrations in support of the victims across France on 11 January, and by the eight million copies of the 'Survivor's Edition' sold. Against its will, *Charlie Hebdo* risked being transformed into an extremely ill-fitting metonym for French identity in the world. Such a burden was utterly inappropriate, but the scale of the global coverage of its plight militated for such an amalgamation. What risked going missing in such global takes on the newspaper was any attempt to get to grips with the nuances of the newspaper and the polyphonic diversity of its content.

The second set of tensions to emerge concerned how freedom of expression as a value could be ethically evaluated given the harm caused to the journalists and the offence *Charlie Hebdo's* satire had courted. This defiantly self-declared 'irresponsible newspaper' was firmly on the side of the ethics of conviction within Max Weber's antagonistic ethical categories for taking into reasonable account the likely outcome of one's actions (the ethics of responsibility), as opposed to following the imperative to voice fully one's convictions within an open arena of debate (for a more detailed explanation see Weber, 1946). *Charlie Hebdo* had always defended its satire as an act of freedom of conscience and had argued that those in disagreement with its material had only not to buy the newspaper. The ethics of responsibility, by contrast, militates against speech liable to create friction, with concern for safety as its corollary. It is easy to see how the satire and provocative humour of the type favoured by *Charlie Hebdo* could fall foul of such an imperative. It is from the ethics of responsibility that the credo 'Je suis Charlie, but...' would easily emerge.

Charlie Hebdo's anticlerical verve was in fact inscribed in a tradition dating back to the French revolution and the drive to remove Catholicism from the sphere of influence of the French state. Notably, since September

11 2001, it had extended its anticlericalism to Islamic extremism as an ideology to critique on an equal footing with Judaism or Christianity, in what it argued was the opposite of racism. A key part of *Charlie Hebdo's* aesthetic and thematic heritage was its highly provocative, Juvenalian satire that broadsided all manners of 'sacred' or sensitive topics on principle. Its founder, François Cavanna, had indeed described such 'stupid and vile' humour as a defence mechanism against absurdity, and a healthy impulse in the face of the violence and stupidity to be witnessed throughout the history of humanity (see Cavanna, 1982).

One early sign of the newspaper turning, in the UK context, from a totem of freedom of expression into a taboo, was when the French journalist and essayist Caroline Fourest, a former contributor to *Charlie Hebdo*, was cut off live on Sky News on January 15 2015. She had tried to show viewers the green front cover of the 'Survivor's Edition' of January 14 with its depiction of Muhammad holding a 'Je suis Charlie' sign beneath the caption 'All is forgiven'. The scramble by Sky News to apologise for any offence caused epitomised the Anglophone media's anxieties over showing visual depictions of Muhammad that had begun with the violent protests in various Islamic countries in the context of the Danish caricature affair in early 2006. The BBC, notably, in line with the ethics of responsibility, had established a policy of not showing the *Jyllands-Posten's* specially commissioned caricatures of Muhammad but only discussing their content, out of concern for cultural sensitivity. In accordance with the ethics of conviction, *Charlie Hebdo* had condemned such reticence, arguing that without access to the images, citizens would not be able to make an informed opinion or enter into frank debate on the matter, slamming such moves to self-censor as profoundly anti-democratic.

For UK French Studies too, *Charlie Hebdo* had become increasingly associated with flouting the ethics of responsibility for persisting in caricaturing Muhammad and Islam. Notably, one of *Charlie Hebdo's* most virulent critics – and a former contributor to the newspaper – Olivier Cyran, was invited to the University of Manchester on January 30 2015 where he critiqued the paper's editorial line on Islam as contributing to victimising France's North African immigrant populations (Cyran, 2015). While his take on *Charlie Hebdo* fitted well with the self-censorship imperatives of the ethics of responsibility that now tend to dominate the humanities in the UK, Cyran had in fact received some fierce pushback for his claims of racism in *Charlie Hebdo* in France. A Moroccan contributor to *Charlie Hebdo*, sociologist of religion Zineb El Rhazoui, had notably chastised Cyran:

> *Charlie Hebdo* is truly on the side of anti-racism by opening up its columns to people like me, who can only express themselves in their countries at the risk of imprisonment or violence, as opposed to you, who would have the whole 'Muslim race' at the mercy of its self-proclaimed clergy. (El Rhazoui, 22/12/13)

In a safety-first climate, in which tensions were further heightened by a gunman attack at a freedom of speech event in Copenhagen on February 14th 2015, the move to block academic discussion of *Charlie Hebdo* was an extension of the unease over the ethics of responsibility with regards to the magazine's material. It was probably also fuelled by a rush to establish professional critical distance from the emotiveness of the #jesuischarlie phenomenon. The first academic event to run into trouble was a symposium to be held on June 4th – 5th at Queen's University, Belfast: 'Understanding Charlie: New perspectives on contemporary citizenship after *Charlie Hebdo*'. The call for papers evoked the 'powerful divisions in global opinion' that had arisen from the 'survivor's edition' of *Charlie Hebdo*, inviting participants to assess critically freedom of speech in a global context, the role of self-censorship, and the place of satire in a multicultural setting. It is ironic that discussion topics so attuned to the ethics of responsibility were judged too toxic – and dangerous – by the university's Vice Chancellor to host due to 'the security risk for delegates and the reputation of the university', as participants were informed in May by email.

The symposium's keynote speaker, Professor Brian Klug, publicly condemned the cancellation, as did Index on Censorship Chief Executive Jodie Ginsberg, who argued:

> If all public discussion on important issues is shut down because of security fears then the terrorists have won. Free speech – including the free exchange of ideas – is vital for democracy and universities in particular should be the torch bearers for free expression. (in Reidy, 21/04/15)

The cancellation would have held had it not been for one of the symposium participants, journalist and PhD candidate Jason Walsh, widely alerting the media. Walsh aptly commented:

> The only conceivable reason this conference would be cancelled is that someone – someone like me, for

instance – might say something that might upset someone else. That is what passes for reputational damage today? Back when I was knee-high to a parking meter we called that debate, and isn't that what the university is all about? (Walsh, 20/04/15)

Walsh's sense that *Charlie Hebdo* and freedom of speech as topics had been deemed too much of a risk owing to the offence they might cause again evokes the influence of an overweening fear of flouting the ethics of responsibility.

While the symposium ultimately went ahead following a media backlash, it felt a pyrrhic victory for any future academic events on *Charlie Hebdo*. Three types of security guard patrolled the venue and a guard was present in the symposium lecture theatre at all times. Such intense security measures served to brand Charlie Hebdo as inherently toxic, financially costly and physically dangerous to engage with as an academic topic.

Prior to the Belfast symposium, I was informed that a second set of academic papers on *Charlie Hebdo* had been cancelled on security grounds. On January 16, the organiser of 'Voyages: 2015 Graphic Novel and Bande Dessinée Conference', to be held at the University of London in Paris (ULIP), had invited additional papers on *Charlie Hebdo* in an extended call for papers 'due to the recent events in Paris and their relevance to the study of comic art/bande dessinée' (French language graphic novels). On May 20th 2015, the conference organiser, Catriona MacLeod, contacted the event's *Charlie Hebdo* panellists to inform them that owing to concerns over the use of the building, which was shared with the British Council, the management of ULIP and the British Council were cancelling the panels in order to safeguard the young learners who also used the ULIP premises (as reported in *Actualitté* 01/06/15 and *Charlie Hebdo* 03/06/15). As such, she asked if speakers would be willing to contribute on a different topic.

As a specialist on *Charlie Hebdo*, I was entirely unwilling to do so. The two *Charlie Hebdo* panels, which included a diverse range of perspectives, already had a discrete place in the programme (panel 30: *Charlie Hebdo* 1: The Ethics of Representation and panel 35: *Charlie Hebdo* 2: *Charlie Hebdo* and the French Republic). Panel 30 had included my paper, 'Political cartooning in *Charlie Hebdo*: joyful resistance versus the ethics of responsibility', a paper by Kenan Koçac entitled 'What is wrong with caricaturing the Prophet Muhammad for Muslims?' and Zanne Lyttle: 'Presenting the "Unrepresentable": drawings of God in comics long before *Charlie Hebdo*'. Panel 35 was to have had a presentation by Olivier Morel: 'Drawing conclusions? The attack on *Charlie Hebdo* in France's long history' and Guillaume de Syon: '*Volez sur* Air Con: *Charlie Hebdo* as social critique of supersonic transport in the 1970s'. Some of these papers could easily have been included on panels with a different name.

I was all the more surprised at the cancellations given that the Belfast symposium had recently been reinstated, Queen's University having been effectively shamed into backing down. I decided to try to challenge such de facto censorship and trampling of academic freedom, replying that I found the move utterly disproportionate and that I would count on voicing the matter as widely as possible within the academic community and beyond.

I was to discover that cohabiting with the British Council had made ULIP subject to safety concerns extending far beyond the normal limitations of what one would expect for a university. This type of hybrid institution fits the increasing 'specialisation' of universities into diverse institutional formats with the 'marketisation' of the UK higher education sector (see, for example, Molesworth, Nixon and Scullion, 2011).

In my attempt to appeal against the cancellation I contacted Paul Docherty and the Vice Chancellor of the University of London, Sir Adrian Smith. I tried to advocate for academic freedom by evoking the ideal of universities since the Middle Ages as places of safety where regardless of outside politics, debates could be held and ideas exchanged. My central point to Paul Docherty, which was posted on *Francofil*, a moderated electronic discussion forum for academics working in the discipline of French Studies and hosted by Liverpool University, on 30th May 2015, was as follows:

> There seems to have been a profound value judgment made, per se, on the basis of the two panels of the conference having '*Charlie Hebdo*' in their titles. If the panels had been called 'Freedom of Expression', would the same danger have been deemed to exist? [...] Are the parents aware that their children are the justification for your spirit of precaution, and hitherto unspecified risks assessed in a hitherto unspecified fashion? [...] I can moreover only reiterate my profound concern as to how disproportionate this move appears, based solely on the criteria of location. ULIP and the British Council are at Invalides. Close to the Ecole Militaire, next to the Ministry of Foreign Affairs and the Assemblée Nationale, in the very heart of Paris. The premises are known not primarily as a creche or a primary school but as the home of the British Council as a cultural ambassador of the UK in France. I would also stress that if you truly are

aware of a specific threat it needs to be made known in concrete terms. (Weston Vauclair, posting to *Francofil*, 30/05/15)

The conference organisers at ULIP suggested moving the panels to an unspecified outside location, an offer which was acceptable for one speaker, ignored by two panellists and rejected by two further speakers, including myself, on the grounds that such a move would seal the marginalisation of the topic from the rest of the conference. By now, news of the cancellation of the conference sessions had spread beyond academia. Along with the French literary news website, *Actualitté*, *Charlie Hebdo* itself covered the story, its editor in chief Gérard Biard commenting on June 3rd 2015:

> This isn't the first time a university has looked to cancel debate on *Charlie* and on freedom of expression. Just this April, Queen's University Belfast also set out to bury a university conference on the topic, before changing its mind after an academic outcry.

> But, true to form, the Englishman won't budge. The British Council has proved inflexible, in the name of security, particularly of the young students taking classes next to the site. Magnanimous, and because the British Council is of course attached to freedom of expression, it nevertheless suggests to the participants of these two high-risk round tables to go off and do their silly things further away, elsewhere, in the cellar, in the attic or on the moon, whatever they feel like.

> The British Council is of course responsible for the safety of the children on its premises. But this honourable cultural institution is also responsible

for ensuring these students can grow up and live in a world of rich and varied cultures and worthwhile debate. And anticipating the desires of obscurantist fanatics who only use violence and terror as arguments is not necessarily the best way to achieve it. (Biard, 03/06/15, my translation),

Actualitté, a French literary news website, meanwhile referred to the event as having been covered in a 'strange, chaste veil', and asked who had really been behind the decision to cancel the panels (Solym, 01/06/15).

On 30th May 2015 I asked French Studies academics on *Francofil* for their perspectives on the cancellation, stressing:

> Despite what Mr Docherty is claiming, cancelling the panels is *not* the only option, in my opinion. Hosting any event carries risks - that doesn't mean that we simply stop hosting events. Rather, we take steps to *mitigate* risks, for example, we increase the security presence/procedures at the event. In this case, there is a choice between mitigating risks in a way that tramples on our values of free expression, or mitigating risks in a way that does *not* trample on those values. (Weston Vauclair, posting to *Francofil*, 30/05/15)

One respondent to my question, Professor Andrew Knapp of Reading University, defended Paul Docherty's position on 31st May 2015, evoking the risks of terrorist attacks and the imperative to take responsible measures, but not the possibility of mitigating such risks through other channels than blocking the panels:

> Mr Docherty [has] a choice. It involves balancing the mission of ULIP and of the British Council, to which free speech is essential, and his responsibility

to ensure that armed men do not walk into the building, which as you know gives directly onto the rue de Constantine, and start shooting, whether on the day of the conference or at any later date. I am not certain how free he is to make this choice alone. (Knapp, posting to *Francofil*, 31/05/15)

However, Dr Gillian Ni Cheallaigh of King's College London countered:

We can do nothing, in reality, to prevent someone who is determined to carry out a violent attack based on extremist ideology. Does that mean that we start to adjust our behaviour, a little more and more with each attack, to concede to the extremist position they feel justifies their attack and that makes our lifestyle subject to attack? [...] Do we start to muzzle healthy open free debate and discussion - for which we have fought for centuries – 'in case' we might upset those who disagree with us? If so, the battle is lost. Hate, intolerance, violence, prejudice and theocratic extremism have won. ULIP is a university. A university is a site and institution devoted and dedicated to the dissemination and encouragement of knowledge, openness, learning and understanding. To cancel, remove or displace this panel is to send the young people in this educational establishment the worst possible signal. It would be to signal that intolerance and violence, or the threat of violence, are powerful and victorious. How awful. We can do nothing to deter determined radical extremists. Except persevere with upholding and practising our values of tolerance, openness, debate and understanding. Are these values not those which drove us towards the humanities in the first place? (Ni Cheallaigh, posting to *Francofil*, 31/05/15)

Keith Reader, Emeritus Professor at ULIP, equally voiced his support on the matter on 2nd June 2015:

> Qua visiting emeritus at ULIP I should like to make plain my anger at what seems to me to be the quite exaggerated reaction of the British Council to the inclusion of papers on CH [*Charlie Hebdo*] at the upcoming Voyages conference. The possible presence of children on the premises – though presumably not at the conference – appears an extremely weak alibi for a frankly pusillanimous attitude. If these papers are removed from the programme, those seeking to silence debate will effectively have won. (Reader, posting to *Francofil*, 02/06/15)

Many members of the public also wrote in to both Paul Docherty and the Chief Executive Officer of ULIP, Tim Gore, who looked to minimise the impact of the cancellations in his replies to these messages. His response has been published on an internet blog:

> Despite the cancellation of a small number of presentations on security grounds, these conferences will allow participants to debate on a wide range of themes related to bande dessinée, from the Middle Ages to the present day, including the *Charlie Hebdo* affair and the unprecedented events that took place last January in Paris. (See Solheim, 12/06/15)

The fact that Gore reassured people that *Charlie Hebdo* could be discussed freely at the event tended again to reinforce the sense that what was substantially left was a simple taboo: the words '*Charlie Hebdo*' in the title of the conference papers. For the conference itself, two measures were ultimately decided upon in mitigation of the cancellations, which were not revoked. Firstly, the affected panellists co-authored a statement, which was expected to appear in the conference programme, but in fact only featured in the book of abstracts. It stated:

> While the organizers and the panellists recognize that matters of security for all members of the public (not just conference participants) is of utmost importance, they regret this decision. They should like to note that, ironically, the very ostracization of the *Charlie Hebdo* panels may prompt participants to talk about this periodical, its impact and meaning far more than originally intended. The panels' absence and unspeakability echo the absence of the cartoonists and journalists lost through the original killings in January.

> (De Syon, Lyttle, Morel, Weston Vauclair, 2015)

Secondly, an 'online panel' was organised as a Facebook discussion group. This group was sparsely attended (thirteen participants, half of whom were not conference delegates). It was entirely unsatisfactory as a replacement for a conference panel, encouraging participants to merge their personal and professional identities and to leave a far more permanent trace of their reasoning by working through social media. The move did however show the degree of acrobatics the organisers were prepared to go to in order to try and mitigate the initial cancellation.

Moves to cancel academic debate on *Charlie Hebdo* show how malignant levels of concern for the ethics of responsibility can result in difficult but important topics being turned into taboos. The Belfast conference was rendered financially exorbitant by the security costs incurred through the decision to demonstrate the extreme risk the topic represented. At the Paris conference, the organisers thanked the British Council for hosting the event for free – but at what cost to academic freedom? *Charlie Hebdo* has no business being turned into a taboo as a topic. The newspaper has a rich and complex history and should not remain victim to global reductionism of its identity via the shattering force of the #jesuischarlie media event and its afterlives.

References

Biard, G. (2015) 'Charlie sujet de débat interdit' in *Charlie Hebdo* (03/06/15).

Cavanna, F. (1982) *Bête et Méchant*, Paris: Belfond.

Cyran, O. (2015) Presentation at 'Are We Charlie?' roundtable discussion held at Manchester University. Transcript available at: http://documents.manchester.ac.uk/display.aspx?DocID=23785 (accessed 04/12/15).

El Rhazoui, Z. (2013) 'Si *Charlie Hebdo* est raciste, alors je le suis' (22/12/13). Available at http://www.cercledesvolontaires.fr/2013/12/22/si-charlie-hebdo-est-raciste-alors-je-le-suis-reponse-de-zineb-el-rhazoui-a-olivier-cyran/ (accessed 04/12/15).

Koçak, K., Lyttle, Z., Morel, O., De Syon, G., and Weston Vauclair, J., (2015) '*Charlie Hebdo* Panels', Statement in 'Book of Abstracts' for Voyages conference, University of London Institute in Paris, June 2015.

Luz (2015) 'Tout le monde nous regarde, on est devenu des symboles' in *Les Inrocks* (10/01/15). Available at http://www.lesinrocks.com/2015/01/10/actualite/luz-tout-le-monde-nous-regarde-est-devenu-des-symboles-11545315/ (accessed 04/12/15).

Molesworth, M., Scullion, R., and Nixon, E. (eds.) (2011), *The Marketisation of Higher Education and the Student as Consumer,* London: Routledge.

Riedy, P. (2015) 'Queen's University Belfast cancels *Charlie Hebdo* conference, citing security fears' in *Little Atoms* (21/04/15). Available at http://littleatoms.com/queens-university-belfast-cancels-charlie-hebdo-conference (accessed 04/12/15).

Seymour, R. (2015) 'On *Charlie Hebdo*' in *Jacobinmag* (01/01/15). Available at https://www.jacobinmag.com/2015/01/charlie-hebdo-islamophobia/ (accessed 04/12/15).

Solheim, J. (2015) 'On banning discussion of *Charlie Hebdo* at academic conferences' (30/05/15). Available at: http://jennifersolheim.com/2015/05/30/on-banning-discussion-of-charlie-hebdo-at-academic-conferences (accessed 04/12/15).

Solheim, J. (2015) 'Update on *Charlie Hebdo* censure from the IBDS conference at ULIP' (12/06/15). Available at http://jennifersolheim.com/2015/06/12/update-on-charlie-hebdo-censure-from-the-ibds-conference-at-ulip/ (accessed 04/12/15).

Solym, C. (2015) 'Qui veut museler la Conférence sur les romans graphiques et les comics?' in *Actualitté* (01/06/15). Available at https://www.actualitte.com/article/bd-manga-comics/charlie-hebdo-victime-d-une-censure-universitaire/58704 (accessed 04/12/15).

Walsh, J. (2015) 'The tragic irony of censoring Queen's University's *Charlie Hebdo* discussion' in Little Atoms (20/04/15). Available at: http://littleatoms.com/society/tragic-irony-censoring-queens-universitys-charlie-hebdo-discussion (accessed 04/12/15).

Weber, M. (1946) [1919] 'Politics as a Vocation', in H. H. Gerth and C. Wright Mills (eds), Max Weber: *Essays in Sociology*, New York: Oxford University Press.

Safe Space Rhetoric Versus Real Violence

Jason Walsh

In the romantic imagination, universities are still thought of as the greatest redoubt of free speech, a 'safe space' where students are exposed to difficult material, and where researchers and scholars subject all manner of ideas to the white heat of debate. According to this vision, no idea is too outrageous for scholarly interrogation and none, no matter how bovine, is sacred.

In reality, universities today are hotbeds of censorship. Student activists have banned controversial speakers and a society dedicated to discussing philosophy (Jacobson, 2015); they have forbidden the sale of a tabloid newspaper (Preskey, 2013) and demanded so-called 'trigger warnings' on key canonical texts. Instead of challenging student-censors, scholars complain that both the dead hand of market economics – invariably referred to as 'neo-liberalism' – and excessive government intervention in education are threats to academic freedom.

All too often academics ignore the far more insidious attacks upon academic freedom that emerge from within rather than from outside of universities. They miss the less explicit and more pervasive threats because they fail to make the connection between freedom of speech in society at large and their own right to pursue research free from government-sanctioned interference. Any defence of academic freedom that does not also support more general free speech rights is narrow, partial and confused.

One result of this confused approach to academic freedom can be seen in the response of scholars to the *Charlie Hebdo* massacre of January 7, 2015. While many members of the public took to the internet to defend free speech it is difficult to escape the conclusion that scholars manned the barricades on the other side, defaming the newspaper and seeking to contextualise the murders as a result of the actions of the French polity.

One multi-authored post on The Immanent Frame, a website whose purpose is to publish 'interdisciplinary perspectives on religion, secularism, and the public sphere' was particularly revealing: writing there, anthropologist Sindre Bangstad, a theology researcher at the University of Oslo, warned of the 'risk of turning the libertarian-anarchist *soixante-huitards* of *Charlie Hebdo* into martyrs in a liberal free speech pantheon through liberal media megaphones [feeding] the flames of stigmatization and polarization in contemporary Europe' (17/02/15). Meanwhile, Amelie Barras, assistant professor of social science at York University in Canada, took the opportunity to complain of the French state (which has nothing to do with *Charlie Hebdo*) using *laïcité* as 'justification to scrutinize and interfere with the bodies, sensibilities, and practices of Muslim citizens (particularly women)' (The Immanent Frame, 17/02/15) while Vincent Lloyd, assistant professor of religious studies at Georgia State University, wrote: 'Charlie is the class clown, the masculine performed' (The Immanent Frame, 17/02/15).

Jocelyne Cesari, a senior research fellow at Georgetown University and director of the Islam in the West programme at Harvard University, said the targeting of *Charlie Hebdo* was a 'response to the broader French political and cultural environment that has been growing more and more hostile toward Islam' (The Immanent Frame, 17/02/15). Grace Davie, a sociologist at the University of Exeter, wrote of the 'obvious similarity between the visual representations' in *Charlie Hebdo's* images of Muslims to Nazi anti-Semitic propaganda (The Immanent Frame, 17/02/15). Tariq Modood, a fellow sociology professor at the University of Bristol, also raised the spectre of the Nazis and wrote the 'argument has not really been about the right to free speech but about how to exercise the responsibility that goes with free speech' (The Immanent Frame, 17/02/15).

Elsewhere, political theorist Jacob Levy took to the BBC to warn of a 'backlash' and complain of the hypocrisy of the French state banning the niqab, arguing it itself was an assault on freedom of expression. 'The deep structural context for the Paris massacres is not irrelevant,' wrote political scientist Patricia Springborg, (Springborg, 2015, p. 19). US-based fellow political scientist Norman Finkelstein said: '*Charlie Hebdo* is not satire. It is sadism' (in Caglayan, 19/01/15). American philosopher Jason Stanley wrote in *The New York Times*: 'To mock the pope is to thumb one's nose at a genuine authority, an authority of the majority. To mock the Prophet Muhammad is to add insult to abuse' (Stanley, 08/01/15). Irish law professor Neville Cox said *Charlie Hebdo* was hate speech and congratulated the French state for also planning to 'come down really hard on anti-semetic speech' [sic], suggesting it should do the same for anti-Islamic sentiment (in McGreevy, 16/02/15). Oxford University philosopher Brian Klug wrote that the public, outraged at the massacres, 'don't know their own minds' on the matter of free speech (Klug, 11/01/15). On this he has a point, but the fact remains that free speech includes the right to publish grossly offensive material.

French sociologist and historian Emmanuel Todd's latest book, *Qui est Charlie? Sociologie d'une crise religieuse* (in English entitled *Who is Charlie?: Xenophobia and the New Middle Class*) makes the apparent claim that the demonstrations on the streets in Paris that occurred in the wake of the *Charlie Hebdo* massacre were xenophobic, authoritarian and nationalist in nature. No doubt further scholarly work is in progress, in English as well as in French, but Todd's is noteworthy because it is in line with much of the non-Francophone reading of events privileged in the academy.

This response, expressing fear of reprisals against Muslims, was no doubt well-intentioned. Yet this need for contextualisation rather than condemnation is driven by the very same reflex that students deploy to create 'safe spaces'. Those perceived as victims, in the case of *Charlie Hebdo* not the murdered journalists but Muslim citizens, are placed beyond intellectual challenge. This veneration of victimhood is now threatening academic freedom.

Despite, or perhaps because of, the brief public outpouring of grief over the January 7, 2015 massacre, *Charlie Hebdo* has, among the Anglophone intelligentsia, rapidly been transformed into a whipping boy for the crime of 'liberal racism'. Today it is often assumed that traditional liberal aspirations for universalism serve to flatten the lived experience of various ethnic and immigrant groups. Indeed, in September 2015, another round of *Charlie Hebdo*-bashing got underway, on the basis that a cartoon highlighting a hypocritical response from 'Christian Europe' to drowning Muslim refugees is prejudiced – against Muslims (Hume, 15/09/15). One can only assume *Charlie Hebdo's* cartoon is being wilfully misinterpreted. D. Peter Herbert, chair of Britain's Society of Black Lawyers, threatened to sue the paper. In the International Criminal Court, Herbert described the publication as a 'purely racist, xenophobic and ideologically bankrupt publication that represents the moral decay of France' (Jackson, 16/09/15).

Prior to the murders, *Charlie Hebdo* entered Anglophone consciousness, if at all, only after reprinting the notorious Mohammed cartoons from Danish newspaper *Jyllands-Posten* an act undertaken by many newspapers in continental Europe, but one that would leave *Charlie Hebdo* requiring police protection. The absence of scholarly work in English suggests that this, and this alone, drove the response of Anglophone scholars. It was a response of 'framing', 'context' and 'narratives' borne of a contraction in serious political debate and studiously ignorant not only of the banal facts of events, but also rejecting the liberal universalism of all citizens being not only equal before the law, but also subjected to the same level of public criticism regardless of their position in society. In place of the traditional demand for the freedom to explore ideas was substituted a limited form of 'criticality' focused solely on exposing power imbalances, and the privileging of subtext over text, facilitating the de-emphasis of empirical fact. In this case, the nebulous, but not unreal, context of the *Charlie Hebdo* massacre was privileged over the event itself.

My point is not that Anglophones fail to understand *Charlie Hebdo*, though that is also true (see: Hume, 2015; Walsh, 2015 and Weston Vauclair, 2015), but rather that an assault on freedom of expression is underway in the name of protecting 'vulnerable' minorities. This reaction, though it has since spread far beyond the halls of academe, is couched in the 'critical' language of New Left analyses of power relations. Many of the arguments surrounding *Charlie Hebdo* are not without merit, but the problem is precisely that they surround it; they do not address it. So, *laïcité,* for instance, the French state's policy of is certainly worthy of scrutiny; France's veil ban is an assault on freedom of expression; official French espousal of republican values should be challenged alongside a questioning of the extent of discrimination in the country and France's military adventures abroad, and so on. None of these matters, however, is remotely concerned with the issue at hand with *Charlie Hebdo*: is the right to be offensive to be defended?

Few appear willing to make the a priori case for answering yes. As this chapter shows, the response of scholars to the murder of the *Charlie Hebdo* staff was not driven by a desire to defend the right to be offensive but by the fear of racism. Even those who did not directly charge *Charlie Hebdo* itself with racism made the argument that, contextually, the publication's lampooning of Muslim clerics and the Prophet Muhammad harmed Muslims, either by offending them or by fanning the flames of a feared Islamophobic response by the state or mobs of rampaging individuals.

There is another way of understanding this rush to explain why *Charlie Hebdo* should not have published material offensive to Muslims. It could be the case that preferred identity groups are privileged by an intellectual establishment so dedicated to 'critical' responses to events that events themselves are of little consequence. This perverse response to concrete events is nothing new. As Roger Scruton noted, the critical theorists 'arrived in California to be confronted by the appalling sight of an unalienated working class', only to 'set about to dispel the illusion, producing reams of turgid nonsense devoted to showing that the American people are just as alienated as Marxism requires them to be' (Scruton, 2010, p. 89).

Understanding the scholarly response to the *Charlie Hebdo* massacre requires an understanding of the radically expanded concept of harm. Today, 'vulnerable' groups are considered to need protection through the creation of 'safe spaces' where the expression of ideas is strictly controlled. At the same time, actual violence, up to and including murder, so long as it is performed by members of 'vulnerable' groups, is explained away as an unfortunate, but predictable, response to provocation and offence. Various intellectual currents, from post-colonial theory to critical theory and post-structuralism are brought together into an intellectual bricolage that starts from the point of view that liberal universalism, now a mere Western illusion, is in actuality a Trojan horse for racism, imperialism, sexism, Islamophobia and other effrontery to the politics of identity forged in oppression. Emotional distress, therefore, becomes both a cause of oppression and an effect of it.

The traditional liberal view of the relationship between freedom of action, including expression, and the use of power to stop actions was exemplified by John Stuart Mill's 'harm principle'. Mill argued that power can only rightfully be exercised to prevent harm to others (Mill, 2008, p. 14), this specifically excludes notions of emotional harm, which cannot be quantified. Today, this very un-quantifiability forms the basis for demands for censorship. Where Mill called for widespread tolerance of dissent, both because the clash of ideas is how truth is discovered and also because no individual has the right to silence another, today we increasingly hear demands for censorship in the name of rebalancing the scales of justice in society.

Herbert Marcuse's essay *Repressive Tolerance* clearly sets out the argument most frequently heard today: that the influence of power and wealth must be counterbalanced by suppression of views. Marcuse argues: 'Part of this struggle is the fight against an ideology of tolerance which, in reality, favors and fortifies the conservation of the status quo of inequality and discrimination' (Marcuse, 1965, p. 123). This is to suggest that tolerance of divergent opinion must be shut down in the name of tolerance itself.

This plays out today in the banning from university campuses of figures as diverse as radical feminist Julie Bindel; the activist and author Ayaan Hirsi Ali; secularist Maryam Namazie and International Monetary Fund managing director Christine Lagarde. It can also be seen in the Canadian government's attempt to prosecute journalist Mark Steyn for 'hate speech', the student-led banning of *The Sun* newspaper from British university campuses, and the campaigns against the pop song *Blurred Lines* on the basis that it promotes an alleged 'rape culture'. In all of these cases, as with the accusation that *Charlie Hebdo* contributed to a climate of Islamophobia or was itself racist 'hate speech', the central claim is one of psychic or emotional oppression.

The banning of feminists from speaking at university campuses – primarily radical feminists who oppose transgender politics, but more recently also secularist figures such as Maryam Namazie – occurs because of a shifting hierarchy of victimhood and, therefore, the construction of a complex series of protections. Viewed through this prism, women are oppressed by men, but white women oppress non-white women (and, indeed, men), as well as transgender individuals and so on. Group identity becomes the basis for rights rather than the traditional rights-bearing individual subject, who is recast in the role of a racist, colonialist and patriarchal construction or, in some cases a pure fantasy (see Heartfield, 2006; and Zizek, 1999). If recognition is privileged over freedom, then the entire concept of rights risks degeneration. Rights are no longer expressed by the actions of individuals, but in the protection of group members; hence the clamour for censorship.

This tendency to valorise the underdog is recognisable throughout history. Indeed, in 1950 Bertrand Russell noted it in the politics of the French Revolution (Russell, 2009, p. 57). However, there is no question that arguments of identity and recognition have taken on a new urgency since the rise of the New Left in the 1960s and, in particular, its rising influence in politics, the law and, most obviously, the academy. Consequently, the right to freedom of expression is now weighed against an apparent right to not be offended, with offence directly mapped to oppression and, in radical versions of the thesis, psychosomatic, and even somatic, harm.

Not only is emotional oppression an unquantifiable standard, it is used, perversely, to reframe acts of censorship as acts promoting free speech. A victimised group is silenced by having less power than those who oppose it, thus the silencing of its opponents is transmuted from what it is, censorship, into its opposite: promoting freedom of expression. Nowhere in this account of expression is the power of oppressed and disadvantaged individuals and groups to band together and form their own forums, and indeed presses, as did New York's immigrant Jews in the nineteenth century (to give but one example) when they founded publications such as *Forverts* (*The Jewish Daily Forward*) and *Freie Arbeiter Stimme* (*The Free Voice of Labour*).

At the heart of this worldview is a further assault on the individual: the belief that individuals, now recast as mere group members, do not possess the intellectual, moral or emotional resources to deal with competing ideas. Thus, those who claim membership of sanctioned vulnerable groups are likely to be damaged by the expression of ideas, whereas those who are not members of sanctioned vulnerable groups are in danger of acting as a mob as a result of encountering ideas.

Despite complaints from scholars about the student-led banning of individuals like Namazie (and at the time of writing, feminist luminary Germaine Greer) from university campuses, the students leading these campaigns are simply putting into practice the ideas they have learned in the seminar room. It was the post-colonialist scholars who saw only racism in Western culture; it was the feminist scholars who saw the freely-willing individual as a patriarchal construct that imprisons women, and so on. Likewise, the intellectual assault on *Charlie Hebdo* misses the fact that *Charlie Hebdo's* politics itself are those of the *soixante-huitard* generation. Scholars defaming *Charlie Hebdo* are, knowingly or not, simply using the ideas of the New

Left against itself. The main target of *Charlie Hebdo's* ire, after all, was not Muslims but the French right.

With the relativists' ghostly thumb on the scales of justice, scholars are now arguing not for a dictatorship of the proletariat, but for a dictatorship of the doctorates. In all of their apparent defences of the vulnerable, the primary objection could be said to be to the public itself en masse. As with nineteenth century critics of the penny press, the real fear appears to be one of the masses bypassing the cultural elites.

Thus academics have been at the forefront of promoting vulnerability, often using it as a lever to silence those who defend freedom of expression a priori, often in the name of radical or, paradoxically, liberal politics. Scholars have challenged key liberal concepts such as universality and the very nature of rights, concepts that belong at the heart of the university experience. The response to *Charlie Hebdo* is little more than a footnote in this wider culture war, but it is indicative of the prevailing privileging of communitarian and therapeutic impulses that seek to dethrone the individual as the locus of action and reasoning as the bedrock upon which these actions stand.

Without a commitment to reason there is no point to dialogue at all. In the brave new world where offence is often perceived to be a greater harm than being shot in the head, it is not only newspapers, satirical or otherwise, that should pack up and go home, but the liberal arts themselves. Thus all debate, and ultimately civil society, is threatened by the expanding empire of harm, an empire that sees the free-willing individual not as the fulcrum of society and social relations, but as a damaged and damaging toxic element to be contained.

In the name of freedom from some nebulous and ill-defined harm, many in the scholarly world seek to restrict our freedom to live and act as we see fit, free from the encumbrances of bureaucracy and power. So, for all its deconstruction and 'criticality', academia risks unmasking *itself* as an avatar for power. In declaring an almost unread publication as racist, academics claimed to take the side of virtue and of the oppressed, but in doing so they not only promoted an ahistorical reading of *Charlie Hebdo*, they exalted imagined vulnerability over both freedom to act and the very real vulnerability of being murdered by self-appointed censors with guns. The real tragedy is that, as with any attempt at censorship, the end result is the denial of a voice to those who need it most; not the surviving staff of *Charlie Hebdo*, nor even those left afraid to speak up for fear of being murdered or slandered, but those on whose behalf scholars would presume to speak.

Complaints about declining academic freedom in the face of 'neo-liberalism', or even the threats from the newly emboldened Red Guards of the student unions, ring hollow in the halls of an academy that cannot stand up and make a full-throated defence of the right of the public to look at cartoons in a satirical newspaper. If scholars (in receipt of state funding, let it not be forgotten) are not prepared to countenance the parry and thrust of controversial ideas in the wider public sphere, why should anyone concern themselves with their complaints that they feel threatened by government inspectors, official targets or boisterous student commissars?

References

Caglayan, M. (2015) 'Norman Finkelstein: *Charlie Hebdo* is sadism, not satire' in *Andalou Agency Newswire* (19/01/15). Available at: http://www.aa.com.tr/en/politics/norman-finkelstein-charlie-hebdo-is-sadism-not-satire/82824 (accessed 17/09/15).

Heartfield, J. (2006) *The 'Death of the Subject' Explained*. Sheffield: Sheffield Hallam University Press.

Hume, M. (2015) 'Je suis toujours Charlie' in *Spiked* (15/09/15). Available at http://www.spiked-online.com/newsite/article/je-suis-toujours-charlie/17441#.VfqA0otH2Rs (accessed 17/09/15).

Jacobson, H. (2014) 'Nietzsche's ideas might have been dangerous, but that's no reason to ban a club dedicated to the man' in *The Independent* (18/02/15). Available at http://www.independent.co.uk/voices/comment/nietzsches-ideas-might-have-been-dangerous-but-thats-no-reason-to-ban-a-club-dedicated-to-the-man-9535970.html (accessed 11/10/15).

Jackson, M. (2015) 'Has *Charlie Hebdo* gone too far with new cartoons? British lawyers think so' in *The Christian Science Monitor* (16/09/15). Available at: http://www.csmonitor.com/World/Global-News/2015/0916/Has-Charlie-Hebdo-gone-too-far-with-new-cartoons-British-lawyers-think-so (accessed 17/09/15).

Klug, B. (2015) 'The moral hysteria of Je suis Charlie' in *Mondoweiss* (11/01/15). Available at: http://mondoweiss.net/2015/01/moral-hysteria-charlie (accessed 17/09/15).

Marcuse, H. (1965) 'Repressive Tolerance', in *Marcuse.org*. Available at: http://www.marcuse.org/herbert/pubs/60spubs/65repressive tolerance.htm (accessed 09/11/15).

McGreevy, R. (2015) '"*Charlie Hebdo* cartoons linked Islam to terrorism", academic says' in *The Irish Times* (16/02/15). Available at: http://www.irishtimes.com/news/social-affairs/religion-and-beliefs/charlie-hebdo-cartoons-linked-islam-to-terrorism-academic-says-1.2106325 (accessed 17/09/15).

Mill, J.S. (2008) *On Liberty and Other Essays*. Oxford: Oxford University Press.

Preskey, N. (2013) 'Sun set: Now Kingston University bans sale of *The Sun* on campus due to Page 3' in *The Independent* (27/11/13). Available at: http://www.independent.co.uk/student/news/sun-set-now-kingston-university-bans-sale-of-the-sun-on-campus-due-to-page-3-8967598.html (accessed 11/10/15).

Russell, B. (2009) 'The Superior Virtue of the Oppressed' in *Unpopular Essays*. London: Routledge.

Scruton, R. (2010) *The Uses of Pessimism and the Danger of False Hope*. London: Atlantic Books.

Springborg, P. (2015) 'A pencil mightier than a sword?' in *Südtiroler Wirtschaftszeitung*, (16/01/15).

Stanley, J. (2015) 'A Postcard from Paris' in *The New York Times* (08/01/15). Available at: http://opinionator.blogs.nytimes.com/2015/01/08/a-postcard-from-paris/?pagewanted=all (accessed 17/09/15).

The Immanent Frame. (2015) 'Values and violence: Thoughts on *Charlie Hebdo*' in The Immanent Frame (17/02/15) http://blogs.ssrc.org/tif/2015/02/17/values-and-violence-thoughts-on-charlie-hebdo/ (accessed 17/09/15).

Walsh, J. (2015) 'Speak the speech' in *Economia* (12/01/15). Available at: http://economia.ie/ec/2015/speak-the-speech/0112/ (accessed 17/09/15).

Weston Vauclair, J. (2015) 'Local Laughter, Global Polemics: Understanding *Charlie Hebdo*' in *European Comic Art*, 8 (1) pp. 6–14.

Zizek, S. (1999) *The Ticklish Subject: The Absent Center of Political Ontology*. London: Verso.